ASCENT OF MOUNT CARMEL

ASCENT OF MOUNT CARMEL

JOHN OF THE CROSS

Foreword by Claudia Mair Burney

*CONTEMPORARY ENGLISH VERSION
BY HENRY L. CARRIGAN, JR.*

PARACLETE PRESS
BREWSTER, MASSACHUSETTS

Ascent of Mount Carmel

2010 First Printing

Copyright © 2010 by Paraclete Press, Inc.

ISBN 978-1-55725-778-9

Library of Congress Cataloging-in-Publication Data

John of the Cross, Saint, 1542-1591.
   [Subida del Monte Carmelo. English]
   Ascent of Mount Carmel / John of the Cross ; foreword by Claudia
Mair Burney ; contemporary English version by Henry L. Carrigan, Jr.
      p. cm. -- (Paraclete essentials)
   ISBN 978-1-55725-778-9
   1. Mysticism--Catholic Church. I. Carrigan, Henry L., 1954- II.
Title.
   BV5082.3.J64213 2010
   248.2'2--dc22   2010023212

10 9 8 7 6 5 4 3 2 1

Published by Paraclete Press
Brewster, Massachusetts
www.paracletepress.com

Printed in the United States of America

CONTENTS

FOREWORD *by Claudia Mair Burney*   xi

INTRODUCTION   xv

THE STANZAS ON WHICH THIS BOOK IS BASED   3

PROLOGUE   7

BOOK ONE

1 The first stanza is introduced.   11

2 The nature of this dark night.   13

3 The first cause of this night.   13

4 The soul's interior darkness
cannot receive God's light.   16

5 It is necessary for the soul to
journey to God through this
dark night.   20

6 The desires cause two serious evils.   23

7 The desires torment the soul.   25

8 The desires darken and blind the soul.   26

9 The desires defile the soul.   28

10 The desires weaken the soul in
virtue and make it lukewarm.   29

11 The soul that desires to reach divine
union must be free from the slightest desire.   30

12 The desires that suffice to cause these
evils in the soul.   34

13 The way that the soul must follow
in order to enter this night of the senses.   36

14 The second phrase of the stanza is explained.   40

15 The remainder of the first stanza is explained.   41

BOOK TWO

1   The second stanza is introduced.   43

2   The second cause of this night of faith.   45

3   Faith is dark night to the soul.   46

4   The soul must also be in darkness
with respect to spiritual things.   48

5   What is meant by "union of the
soul with God."   50

6   The three theological virtues perfect
the three faculties of the soul.   52

7   The way that leads to eternal life is
narrow.   54

8   Faith is the means by which the soul
may attain to the divine union of love.   58

9   Harm results from the soul not
being able to detach itself from
natural things of the mind.   59

10   The soul must be emptied of
things of the senses.   61

11   The soul must not lean on visions
that take place in the mind.   63

12   Why God allows supernatural
visions.   67

13   Spiritual teachers may lead disciples
into error.   68

14   We may be deceived about visions
and locutions that come from God.   69

15   Why it is not lawful under the law
of grace to ask anything of
God by supernatural means.   74

16   Things of the understanding may
     come in a purely spiritual way.   77

17   Two kinds of spiritual vision that
     come supernaturally.   79

18   The distinction between the
     two kinds of revelation.   82

19   The second kind of revelation is
     the manifestation of hidden secrets.   85

20   Interior locutions may come to the
     spirit in one of three forms.   87

21   The first kind of words that the
     recollected spirit sometimes forms
     within itself.   88

22   The harm that may be done by
     interior words.   91

23   The difference between substantial
     words and formal words.   95

24   The things received by the
     understanding from interior feelings.   97

BOOK THREE

1   The soul must purify the memory
     and the will.   101

2   The soul must be emptied of the
     natural things of the memory.   102

3   Three evils come to the soul when it
     uses natural knowledge and the
     memory.   104

4   The second evil that may come to
     the soul from the natural things
     of the memory.   106

5   The third evil that may come to the soul
through distinct natural
knowledge or the memory.   107

6   The benefits that come to the soul
from emptiness of thoughts and
knowledge.   108

7   One kind of perception of the memory.   109

8   Many evils may come to the soul by
reflecting on supernatural things.   110

9   The peril of falling into self-esteem
and vain presumption.   111

10   An evil that may come to the
soul through imaginary perceptions.   113

11   The hindrance that the soul places
between itself and union.   115

12   Another evil: a low and unseemly
judgment of God.   115

13   The benefits of banishing the
perceptions of the imagination.   117

14   The general method for governing
oneself with respect to the memory.   121

15   The dark night of the will.   122

16   Joy may arise from six kinds of
blessings.   125

17   Joy with respect to temporal blessings.   126

18   The evils that may come to the soul by
rejoicing in temporal blessings.   129

19   The benefits that come to the
soul by withdrawing from joy
in temporal things.   134

20 The evils that may come to the
    soul by rejoicing in the good
    things of nature.   136

21 The benefits that come to the
    soul by not rejoicing in the good
    things of nature.   138

22 The third good thing in which the
    will may rejoice.   140

23 The benefits that come to the
    soul by not rejoicing in things of
    the senses.   141

24 The fourth kind of good in
    which the will may rejoice.   144

25 The seven evils that may come
    to the soul by rejoicing in moral good.   145

26 The benefits that come to the soul
    through not rejoicing in moral good.   148

27 The fifth kind of good in which the
    will may rejoice.   150

28 The evils that come to the soul when
    it rejoices in this kind of good.   152

29 Two benefits that come to the
    soul from renouncing joy in the
    supernatural graces.   156

30 The sixth kind of good in which
    the will may rejoice.   158

31 The spiritual good things that
    bring joy to the will.   159

32 The use of images in perceiving
    God and spiritual things.   161

33   Images can be used to direct
     the soul to God.   164
34   Motives for goodness.   165
35   The way in which oratories and
     churches should be used.   168
36   Three places that God uses to
     move the will to devotion.   170
37   Other motives for prayer that
     many persons use.   172
38   The joy and strength of the
     will must be directed to God
     through devotions.   173
39   Teaching others is a spiritual practice
     rather than a vocal one.   176

I first encountered St. John of the Cross while battling a formidable depression. Many of the writers I loved found him a consoling ally, and through the veil of their works, he comforted me. In their books I discovered "the dark night of the soul" and christened my experience with the same name, mostly because I thought it suited me. I had no idea what the dark night really was, but I can tell you why the enigmatic mystic appealed to me.

St. John of the Cross, like the Savior he adored, was a man of many sorrows, and acquainted with grief. He was persecuted because of his work with St. Teresa of Avila to reform their religious order. Soon his Carmelite brothers confined him to a dank, sixteenth-century prison cell. They let him out only to beat him mercilessly. This gentle soul, more lover than fighter, never recovered from the injuries inflicted on him. Eventually, an infection from one of the old wounds on his leg killed him.

Ironically, while I connected deeply with John of the Cross' suffering, I hadn't actually bothered to read his writing myself. That is, until fibromyalgia and seasonal affective disorder slammed me hard. I couldn't find God if I had a map charting my course directly to heaven. I needed some reliable guides through my maze of pain, allies who had known this kind of night. Then I remembered John of the Cross, and desperately sought out his poetry. I found this ardor-filled verse in *The Spiritual Canticle*:

"Where have you hidden yourself,
abandoning me in my groaning, my Beloved.
You fled like a deer after wounding me.
I ran after you, weeping; but you were gone."

Be still my heart! He'd created his own version of the Song of Songs, and there was more. From his dark night of the soul emerged these lines:

"On a dark night, aroused in love with yearnings—
oh, happy chance!—
I went out without being observed, since all in my
house were asleep."

John of the Cross wrote about being concealed in darkness, having no light except the one, "burning in my Heart." Yet, that night was "more lovely than the dawn." It "joined Beloved with Lover, Lover transformed in the Beloved!" This was no mere clinical depression; this was more like the soul's transfiguration. He described a process of being changed by God into someone more beautiful and spiritual than you were before. Not once did he use religious terms. John of the Cross spoke the language of love.

What you hold in your hands is a gift, my friends, and if you'll allow him to, St. John of the Cross, through this masterful work, *Ascent of Mount Carmel*, will take you on an unforgettable journey. In these pages, like the romantic he is, he's reaching for your hand, to steal away with you into the night. It's a night of stark contrasts: the black darker than midnight, and the bright light more radiant than dawn.

I must warn you, the *Ascent of Mount Carmel* is a dangerous journey. You can die on it like a seed that falls to the ground does, then dwells in darkness before it grows and flowers. It's possible that you could lose yourself, in the way one does when lost in glorious ecstasy.

Your wanderings will be costly, for whatever you brought with you when you set out on this trip, John of the Cross will insist that you let go of it. I mean every little thing that keeps you from union with God, and that, you will see, is more than you may have realized.

It's interesting to note that John never finished his discourse on the meaning of his poem in *Ascent of Mount Carmel*. Perhaps he realized that there are some matters of the soul that even his soaring language can't describe, or, just maybe, he laid down his quill to cavort with God. I don't know. This is what I can assure you of, however, if you go the distance on this journey—oh, happy chance that you even have the privilege to!—you will find yourself in the arms of God. It's a good place to be, my friends. Not everyone makes it there. Don't go there.

Traveling mercies. Accept God's grace.

—*Claudia Mair Burney*

INTRODUCTION

Thomas Merton called John of the Cross "the greatest of all mystical theologians." Merton's judgment is certainly accurate, for John's writings—along with those of Teresa of Avila, Meister Eckhart, and Hildegard of Bingen—continue to offer illuminating spiritual counsel for twenty-first century spiritual pilgrims.

Although John's struggles to reach spiritual union with the Divine occurred within the context of the Christian faith, he uses philosophical and spiritual language in his mystical writings that would appeal to people of all faiths. Indeed, John's ability to focus in an orderly and systematic fashion on the self's stripping itself of all worldly attachments and distractions in order to lose itself in the Divine makes his work even more appealing.

When Pope Pius XI made John a Doctor of the church, he wrote, "He points out to souls the way of perfection as though illumined by light from on high, in his limpid, clear analysis of mystical experience. Although his works discuss difficult and hidden matters, they are nevertheless replete with such lofty spiritual doctrine and are so well adapted to the understanding of those who study them that they can rightly be called a guide and handbook for the person of faith who proposes to embrace a life of perfection."

The life of perfection is not an easy one to embrace, according to John's writings. The soul that wishes to reach divine union, or union with the Beloved, must actively submit itself to a dark night of the senses. In this night, the soul willingly detaches itself from all sensual desires, for such desires impede the progress of the soul on its journey. Once the soul has passed through this night, it finds itself in the night of faith, where it must give up its knowledge and understanding in order to embrace God's love, knowledge, and understanding. Finally, once the soul has given up both sensual and rational desires, God begins his active work of grace as the soul gives itself up to him. Though the journey is arduous, the divine union is blissful.

John's most famous work, *Dark Night of the Soul*, has perhaps been his most misunderstood. Many religious and nonreligious people use the title phrase to describe a particularly bad moment in their lives. Perhaps they have been through a divorce, the loss of a loved one, or the loss of a job, and they struggle with despair and depression as a result. Yet this use of the phrase is not what John had in mind. He experienced his own "dark night of the soul" when he was in prison and felt as if God had abandoned him. On release from his jail cell he found God waiting for him as if a bright light were waiting for him at the end of a long road. John realized then that God was in his dark night all along and had been guiding him to direct his will toward union with God. So, for John, the "dark night of the soul" is not simply a time of unrelieved suffering but one of the aspects of God's love.

John's *Ascent of Mount Carmel* is his introduction of the theme of the dark night. Both works are spiritual commentaries on his poems and "stress the need for active asceticism as well as the far deeper purification of the soul by divine grace and by the unsought humiliations of external agents" (David Hugh Farmer, *The Oxford Dictionary* of Saints, third edition, New York: Oxford, 1992, p. 265). In all his writing, he combines the theological and philosophical rigor of Thomas Aquinas and the spiritual discernment of his contemporary, Teresa of Avila.

BIOGRAPHY

Juan de Yepes y Alvarez was born in the small town of Fontiveros, Spain, in 1542. Although his father was a nobleman by birth, he had been disinherited for marrying a woman below his class. Juan's father died shortly after Juan's birth, leaving the family in poverty. Even so, Juan's mother raised him and made sure that he had an education. He attended a poor-school at Medina del Campo and was apprenticed to a silk weaver. When he showed no aptitude for this trade, he went to a Jesuit college.

When he was twenty-one he joined the Carmelite Order and took the name Juan de la Cruz (John of the Cross). By the time he was twenty-seven he had received a theological education at Salamanca and had been ordained. During this year he was introduced to Teresa of Avila; this meeting proved to be the turning point in his life.

Teresa had been actively trying to reform the Carmelite Order, working to restore it to a simpler and more deeply spiritual community. Teresa's principal concern was that the order did not encourage or honor solitude or poverty, two characteristics she thought absolutely essential to the lives of those seeking perfect contemplation and union with God. By 1571, after she had established the order of Discalced (barefoot) Carmelite nuns, she began to look for a man to establish Discalced Carmelite monasteries for men according to the same patterns of reform. When she met John they both recognized their mutual spiritual affinity.

As their relationship grew deeper, he became not only Teresa's spiritual director but also the first Prior at the community of Discalced Friars in Duruelo. Later in 1571 he became rector of Alcala, a study house that was part of the university, and from 1572 to 1577, he served as confessor to the nuns of Avila.

But the late sixteenth century in Spain was a time of great religious controversy, and John fell victim to the infighting within his own Catholic Church. Many Carmelites disagreed violently with the reform that John and Teresa were carrying out. In 1575, following a general meeting of Calced Friars in Piacenza, John was kidnapped by these unreformed friars and imprisoned in a monastery of theirs in Toledo. These friars treated John poorly, feeding him a diet of bread and water, and beating him regularly. During the time John was in prison he wrote some of his most accomplished and most beautiful poetry. After nine months, when he was close to death, John escaped from the prison under the cover of darkness. This escape provides the central image of the poem, that of the soul slipping out of the house at rest, that opens *Ascent of Mount Carmel*.

Not long after John's escape, the Discalced groups were separated from the Calced groups. He served in a number of capacities from 1579 to 1588. He founded a college at Baeza and served as its rector until 1582. He became Prior at Granada in 1582, the year that Teresa died, and at Segovia in 1588. Even so, in the years after his incarceration John was caught continually in the petty squabbles and jealousies within the Discalced Carmelite order. In 1588 Nicholas Doria, the vicar-general of the Discalced Carmelites, stripped John of his positions and banished him to Ubeda in the province of Andalusia. In Ubeda, a leg wound that John had suffered during his earlier imprisonment became infected. The Prior at the Discalced monastery there disliked John so much that he neglected John's care, and on December 14, 1591, John died in Ubeda, whispering the words: "Into your hands, Beloved, I commend my spirit."

John was beatified in 1675, canonized in 1726, and declared a Doctor of the Church in 1926.

ASCENT OF MOUNT CARMEL

During his imprisonment, John devoted himself to writing astonishing lyrical poetry that captured his spiritual struggles and triumphs. Both *Ascent of Mount Carmel* and *Dark Night of the Soul* are extended treatises on his poetry, *Ascent of Mount Carmel* being the earliest of his spiritual treatises. Although John was probably writing this book at Granada in 1582, he left it incomplete. So he never fully deals with the Night of the Spirit in which God works his grace in our souls as they journey to the Divine.

This spiritual treatise follows the soul on its journey toward perfection, as it purifies itself and passes through the various parts of the dark night of the soul on its way to union with the Divine. John devotes attention to the early stages of the mystical life, realizing that during these stages the soul has its most difficulty throwing off the worldly attachments that hinder its progress to union. In an orderly and systematic fashion, John provides a road map to the soul's journey to the Divine.

In Book One of *Ascent of Mount Carmel*, John emphasizes that in order even to begin this journey to divine union, the soul must purify itself and detach itself from its sensual desires. The soul, because it desires to be in union with God, actively works to cleanse itself from the impurities of the senses and reason. The soul must empty itself of all that is not God to prepare itself to be one with God. According to John, two opposite qualities— God's love and love of worldly things—cannot coexist in the same heart. This purification John calls the "dark night of the senses." This part of the journey is most like midnight because we are plunged into almost total darkness. Not only are we without the light of our senses or our reason to guide us, we are also without the light of God's grace because we are preparing ourselves to receive it.

In Books Two and Three of *Ascent*, John focuses on what he calls the "dark night of faith" or the "dark night of the spirit." Having purified itself from the senses and prepared itself to come into union with God, the spirit must now empty itself of understanding, memory, and will in order to prepare itself to receive the three theological virtues: faith, hope, and love. Just as our senses hinder us from having a pure soul, the understanding hinders us from having a pure spirit. When the soul possesses the three theological virtues, it has moved from meditation to contemplation, that is, from a cerebral engagement with God to a more completely detached union with God.

In Book Three John describes the obstacles to union that the memory and the will present. The earlier chapters explore memory's navigation of the dark night, while the rest describe the ways that the will, moved by love, traverses the dark night. As the will travels this night, joy, hope, sorrow, and fear attack the will, either leading the soul away from the purity of union with God

[handwritten marginal note, left margin:] human will is an obstacle to union with God.

[handwritten note, bottom:] The Protestant theologians do not have "pure spirit" to understand the True Gospel.

or leading it toward its desired divine union. In the third book, John identifies "six kinds of good" that result in rejoicing. Even though he says he will discuss these each in turn, he fails to do so, concentrating instead on a detailed exposition about the rites and rituals of the church.

Since John never completed the treatise, the journey through the "dark night" never reaches its destination, the full light of God's glory and grace. Even so, he provides an illuminating guide for the soul whose most fervent desire is to reach glorious and blissful union with the Divine.

A WORD ABOUT THE TEXT

I have used E. Allison Peers's translation of *Ascent of Mount Carmel* as the basis for the present text. The edition I used comes from an electronic edition found in the Christian Classics Ethereal Library (www.ccel.org). Peers is one of the most respected scholars of Spanish mysticism, and her translations of Teresa of Avila and John of the Cross are literal and faithful to the original texts. Peers's edition also includes helpful biographical information, as well as information about textual variants in the extant manuscripts of *Ascent of Mount Carmel*. Her commentary also provides insight into John's life and work and into the elements of John's engaging writing style.

For biographical information, I have benefited from David Hugh Farmer, *The Oxford Dictionary of Saints*, third edition (New York: Oxford, 1992) and Robert Ellsberg's excellent and inspiring *All Saints: Daily Reflections on Saints, Prophets, and Witnesses for Our Time* (New York: Crossroad, 1997).

Because some of the passages in *Ascent* are repetitive, as they offer a summary of John's arguments in certain sections, I have omitted them. I have also omitted passages that deal particularly with John's religious community since these have too narrow a focus for the general reader. These passages are few and insignificant. This edition contains only Book One of John's *Ascent of Mount Carmel*. Books Two and Three deal with issues particular to his time and community.

I have remained true to the spirit of John's text, even where I have modernized it. Mostly, my modernizations have come in two areas. I have replaced archaic words and forms of address with more modern ones. Thus, "thou" and its related pronoun forms, become "you" and its related forms. I have altered John's syntax and sentence structure to make it livelier and more understandable by a modern audience. Often this simply means casting sentences in the active rather than the passive voice.

The term "recollection" may not be familiar to all readers. Webster defines "recollection" as "quiet tranquility of mind and self-possession, especially religious composure."

Ascent of Mount Carmel offers one of the most enduring and lyrical accounts of the ways in which we can pursue a path that will lead to union with God. John's spiritual directions provide us even today with a map we can follow through our dark nights to bright and glorious union with the Divine.

—*Henry L. Carrigan, Jr.*

ASCENT OF MOUNT CARMEL

This work explains how the soul may prepare itself in order to reach divine union in a short time. It provides profitable instruction to beginners as well as seasoned practitioners so they can know how to free themselves from all that is temporal. It instructs them not to perplex themselves with the spiritual, and to remain in the complete detachment from the world and in the freedom of spirit that are necessary for Divine union.

ARGUMENT

All the doctrine I intend to explore in this *Ascent of Mount Carmel* is included in the following stanzas, and in them I describe the manner of ascending to the summit of the Mount. This summit is the high state of perfection called the union of the soul with God. Because all the arguments I make depend on these verses, I wanted to place the poem here in its entirety so that all my ideas can be seen and understood together. I will sometimes place a stanza at the beginning of a section before explaining it, and discuss individual lines as my argument requires. The poem runs as follows:

THE STANZAS ON WHICH THIS BOOK IS BASED

The soul sings of the happy fortune it had in passing through the dark night of faith, detaching and cleansing itself as it moved to union with the Beloved.

1. On a dark night, aroused in love with yearnings—
   oh, happy chance!—
   I went out without being observed, since all in my
   house were asleep.

2. In darkness and secure, by the secret ladder,
   disguised—oh, happy chance!—
   Concealed and in darkness, since all in my house
   were asleep,

3. In the happy night, in secret, when no one saw me,
   Nor did I see anyone, without light or guide, except
   the light that burned in my
   Heart,

4. This light guided me more surely than the light of
   noon,
   To the place where he (well I knew who!) was
   waiting for me—
   A place where no one appeared.

5. Oh, night that guided me, oh, night more lovely
   than the dawn,
   Oh, night that joined Beloved with Lover, Lover
   transformed in the Beloved!

6. He slept soundly on my flowery breast, which I had
   kept wholly for him alone,
   And I caressed him, and the fanning of the cedars
   made a breeze.

7. The breeze blew from the turret as I parted his hair;
   He wounded my neck with his gentle hand, and
   suspended all my senses.

8. I remained, lost in forgetfulness; I lay my face on the
   Beloved.
   Everything stopped and I abandoned myself,
   forgetting my cares among the lilies.

PROLOGUE

1. I need far greater knowledge and experience than I have to describe this dark night through which the soul passes in order to reach the divine light of the perfect union of God's love. This darkness and these spiritual and temporal trials through which happy souls pass in order to be able to reach this high state of perfection are so numerous and so profound that human knowledge is not fully capable of describing them. The only persons who can describe this dark night are the ones who experience it, and even they cannot describe it accurately.

2. I trust the Lord to help me say a few words that will assist those who have set out on the road of virtue but make no progress as they pass through the dark night to divine union. Sometimes they have no desire to enter this journey; at other times they do not have competent spiritual advisers to guide them. It is sad to see so many souls to whom God gives both aptitude and favor with which to make progress, remaining in an elementary stage of communion with God for lack of will or knowledge, or because there is no one who will lead them in the right path or teach them how to go beyond the beginnings.

3. Although our Lord grants these souls such favor as to make them go onward without obstacles, they arrive at their goal much later and with greater labor, and yet with less merit, because they have neither conformed themselves to God nor

allowed themselves to be brought freely into the pure and sure road of union. They will not allow themselves to be led, so they make less progress because they resist the One who is leading them. They have fewer rewards because they do not apply their will, and because of this they often suffer more. Instead of committing themselves to God and making use of his help, they hinder God by their resistance.

4. In this book, with God's help, I will offer instruction so that seekers can understand God's will and allow him to lead them, for spiritual guides who have no understanding of this experience of the dark night often hinder rather than help seekers on the road to union with the Divine. God will lead the soul by a most lofty path of dark contemplation and dryness of soul, and the soul will seem to be lost. Because of this dark night, some will say that the soul is simply suffering from melancholy or low spirits. Others will say that the soul has been evil so God has forsaken it.

5. Some will tell the soul to start its journey over since it is finding no pleasure or consolation in the things of God as it once did. In this way they double the poor soul's trials. It may well be that its greatest affliction is that of knowing its own miseries and thinking itself full of evils and sins, for God gives it the light of knowledge in the night of contemplation. When a person finds someone whose opinion agrees with his own and who says that these things must be due to his own fault, his affliction and trouble increase infinitely and become more grievous than death.

6. With God's help we will examine the ways the soul should conduct itself during this dark night. We will help the soul

determine whether or not it is experiencing the cleansing of the soul during the dark night of the senses and spirit, or whether this is simply melancholy. Some may think that God is leading them along the road of this dark night of spiritual cleansing, whereas they may possibly be suffering only from some imperfection.

7. Some work hard yet make no progress. Others seek profit in what is not profitable. Still others are disturbed and make no progress precisely because of the favors that God grants so that they may make progress. Yet there are others who make great progress by remaining at rest and in quietness. There are many other things on this road that come to those who follow it—joys and afflictions and hopes and grief. Some come from the spirit of perfection and others from imperfection. We will say something about all these, so that each reader can learn something about the road one should follow to reach the mountaintop.

BOOK ONE

Book One describes the nature of dark night and tells how necessary it is to pass through it to divine union. In particular this book describes the dark night of the senses and the desire and the evils that these work in the soul.

The first stanza is introduced.

"On a dark night, aroused in love with yearnings— oh, happy chance!—I went out without being observed, since all in my house were asleep."

1. In this first stanza the soul sings of the happy fortune it experiences when it succeeds in getting away from the desires and imperfections of human sensuality. For a soul to reach the state of perfection, ordinarily it has to pass first through two principal kinds of night. Spiritual people call these "cleansings" or "purifications of the soul"; in this book we call them "nights," for in both of them the soul journeys, so to speak, by night, in darkness.

12 | *Ascent of Mount Carmel*

The Gospel said Jesus saw His disciples row very hard in the
storm and He meant to pass by them (Mk 6:48)

2.	The first night, or cleansing, is that of the sensual part of
the soul. This we explore in the present stanza and will
explore in the first part of this book. The second stanza
examines the spiritual part of the soul, or the second night.
The second and third parts of the book describe the soul's
activity, and the fourth part of the book describes the soul's
passivity.

This is grace.
Jesus does
not want
His disciples
to row that
hard, He
wanted to
help them.

3.	The first night occurs when God brings new seekers into a
state of contemplation. The second night, or purification,
occurs when God desires to bring more proficient seekers
into union with himself. This second night is a darker and
more terrible cleansing.

4.	In this stanza God is leading the soul that is aroused by
God's love on a journey into the dark night of the cleansing
and purification of all the sensual desires of the flesh and
the will. All of this happens in the cleansing of the senses.
In this stanza the soul says it escaped while the desires in
its house—its sensual part—were asleep. No soul can get
away until the desires are restrained and put to rest. This,
the soul says, was a happy chance for it, that is, going
out without being observed. No fleshly desire was able to
keep the soul from going out.

5.	The happy chance is that God leads the soul into this night,
out of which it gains so much good. By itself the soul could
not have managed this, for no one can succeed in emptying
himself of all desires in order to come to God.

St. John talks about cleansing and purification
in dark night, he totally ignored the sanctification
of the Holy Spirit.

CHAPTER 2
The nature of this dark night.

1. There are three reasons for which the soul's journey to union
    with God is called night. The first has to do with the soul's
    starting point. It must gradually deprive itself of desire for all
    worldly things by denying these things to itself. Such denial
    and deprivation are night to the human senses. The second
    reason has to do with the road along which the soul must
    travel to this union, that is, faith, which also is as dark as night
    to the understanding. The third has to do with the point to
    which it travels—that is, God, who is equally a dark night
    to the soul in this life. The soul must pass through these dark
    nights so that it may come to divine union with God.

2. These three parts of the night are all one, but like actual
    night, they have three parts. The first part, that of the senses,
    can be compared to the beginning of night when things begin
    to fade from sight. The second part, which is faith, can be com-
    pared to midnight, which is total darkness. The third part is like
    the close of night near the light of day, which is God.

When the faith is in total darkness, how can the believer seek the justification by faith only?

CHAPTER 3
The first cause of this night.

1. Night is the lack of every kind of pleasure that pertains to
    the desires. Even as actual night is nothing but the loss of
    light and consequently of all objects that can be seen only

with light, the denial of desire can be called night to the soul. When the soul is deprived of the pleasure of its desire in all things, it remains unoccupied and in darkness. When the soul quenches the pleasure of all things and ceases to desire, pleasure no longer occupies it and it remains in darkness.

2. Here is an example from each of the human faculties: When the soul deprives its desire of the pleasure of all that can delight the sense of hearing, the soul remains unoccupied and in darkness with respect to hearing. When it deprives itself of the pleasure of all that can please the sense of sight, it remains unoccupied and in darkness with respect to sight. When it deprives itself of the pleasure of all the sweetness of perfumes that can give it pleasure through the sense of smell, it remains equally unoccupied and in darkness with regard to the sense of smell. Moreover, if it denies itself the pleasure of all food that can satisfy the palate, the soul remains unoccupied and in darkness. Finally, when the soul restrains itself from all the delights and pleasures it can receive from the sense of touch, it remains, also, unoccupied and in darkness. So the soul that has denied and thrust away from itself the pleasures that come from all these things, and has mortified its desire with respect to them, can be said to be in the darkness of night, which is nothing but emptiness of all things within itself.

3. The reason for this is that as soon as God infuses the soul into the body, the soul is like a smooth, blank board on which nothing is painted. Except for the things that it experiences through the senses, nothing is communicated

to it from any other source. As long as it is in the body, it is like one in a dark prison who knows nothing except what he can see through the prison's windows. So the senses are the prison windows of the soul.

4. If the soul rejects and denies what it receives through the senses, it remains empty and in darkness because no light can enter it by any means other than the windows. One who desires to shut his eyes will remain in darkness, like a blind person who lacks the faculty of sight.

5. For this reason, King David says these words: I am poor and in labors from my youth. He calls himself poor, although he was rich, because his will was not set on riches. So it was as though he were really poor. But if he had not actually been poor in his will, he would not have been truly poor, for his soul, as far as its desire was concerned, would have been rich and full.

6. This kind of detachment from the world is night to the soul, for simply lacking goods does not imply detachment from the world if the soul still desires those goods. Rather, detachment from the world occurs when the desire for such goods leaves the soul free and empty of them. It is not worldly things themselves that occupy the soul or cause it harm—those things cannot enter the soul. It is the will and the desire for them that cause harm.

7. This first kind of night through which the soul must pass to reach union is this dark night of the senses.

CHAPTER 4

The soul's interior darkness cannot receive God's light.

" When I sit in darkness, the Lord will be a light to me. "
(Mc 7:8)

1. The soul must pass through the dark night of the senses because all the passions it feels for created things are pure darkness in God's eyes. When the soul is imbued with the passions, it lacks the capacity for being enlightened and possessed by God's pure and simple light. Light cannot agree with darkness. As John says: The darkness could not receive the light.

2. Two opposite qualities cannot coexist in one person. Darkness, which is passion for created things, and light, which is God, are opposites. As Paul said to the Corinthians: What communion can there be between light and darkness? The light of divine union cannot dwell in the soul if the passions are still present.

3. The passions and attachment the soul has for created things make the soul similar to these created things. The greater the passion, the greater the likeness between them. Love creates likeness between one who loves and the object of its love.

4. One who loves a created thing becomes as low as that created thing, and in some ways lower. Love not only makes the lover equal to the object of his love, but even subjects him to it. In the same way the soul that loves anything else becomes incapable of pure union with God and transformation in him. The low estate of the created

thing is much less capable of union with the high estate of the Creator than is darkness with light.

5. Everything on earth and in heaven compared with God is nothing, as Jeremiah says in these words: I beheld the earth, and it was empty, and it was nothing; I beheld the heavens, and saw that they had no light. When he looked at the heavens and saw no light in them, he says that all the bright stars in the skies, compared with God, are pure darkness. All created things are nothing and their passions are less than nothing, since they are impediments to transformation in God. The soul that expends its passions on created things will not be able to comprehend God, for until it is cleansed it will not be able to possess God, either on this earth through pure transformation of love, or beyond this earth with a clear vision.

6. All the being of creation, then, compared with the infinite Being of God, is nothing. In the same way the soul that spends its passion on the being of creation is nothing in God's eyes, and indeed less than nothing. Love makes for equality and even sets the lover below the object of its love. Such a soul will not in any way be able to reach union with the infinite Being of God.

7. The beauty of created things compared with the infinite beauty of God is the height of deformity, as Solomon says in the Proverbs: Favor is deceitful and beauty is vain. The soul that is passionately attached to the beauty of any created thing is the height of deformity in God's eyes. Therefore this deformed soul cannot be transformed in beauty, which is God, since deformity cannot aspire to beauty. Compared

with God's grace, all the grace and beauty of created things are the height of misery and ugliness. The soul that is ravished by them cannot experience God's infinite grace and loveliness, for that which has no grace is far removed from that which is infinitely gracious.

8. In comparison with God's infinite goodness, the goodness of the created things of the world can be described as wickedness. "For there is nothing good, except only God." Therefore the soul that sets its heart on the good things of the world is supremely evil in God's eyes. Just as wickedness cannot comprehend goodness, such a soul cannot be united with God, who is supreme goodness.

9. All the wisdom of the world and all human ability, compared with God's infinite wisdom, are supreme ignorance. As Paul writes: The wisdom of this world is foolishness with God. Any soul that makes use of its knowledge and ability so it can come to union with God's wisdom is supremely ignorant in God's eyes and will remain far removed from that wisdom. In God's eyes, people who think they have a certain amount of knowledge are ignorant. Only those who lay aside their knowledge to walk in God's service with love acquire God's wisdom. As Paul taught: If anyone among you seems to be wise, let him become ignorant so that he may be wise; for the wisdom of this world is foolishness with God. In order to come into union with God's wisdom, the soul must proceed by unknowing rather than knowing. The dominion and freedom of the world, compared with the freedom and dominion of God's Spirit, is the most abject slavery, affliction, and captivity.

10. The delights and pleasures of the will in the things of the world, in comparison with God's delights, are supreme affliction, torment, and bitterness. One who sets his heart on them is considered in God's sight as worthy of supreme affliction, torment, and bitterness. He will be unable to gain the delights of embracing union with God. Compared to God's wealth, the wealth and glory of creation are supreme poverty and wretchedness. The soul that loves and possesses creature wealth is supremely poor and wretched in God's sight, and for that reason will be unable to gain the wealth and glory that is the state of transformation in God.

11. Divine Wisdom, grieving for such souls who make themselves vile, low, miserable, and poor because they love the things in this world that seem so rich and beautiful, exclaims to them in Proverbs: O you mortals, to you I call, and my voice is to the children of mortals. Attend, little ones, to subtlety and wisdom; you who are foolish, take notice. Hear, for I have great things to speak of. With me are riches and glory, high riches and justice. Better is the fruit that you will find in me than gold and precious stones; and my generation—that is, what you will engender of me in your souls—is better than choice silver. I walk in the ways of justice, in the midst of the paths of judgment, that I may enrich those who love me and fill their treasures perfectly.

12. Here Divine Wisdom speaks to all who set their hearts and passions on anything of the world. She calls them "little ones" because they make themselves like what they love, which is little. Therefore she tells them to be subtle and to take note that she is dealing with great things and not with

little things like themselves, and that the great riches and the glory that they love are with her and in her and not where they think. The wisdom she creates in souls is better than the choice silver that they love.

CHAPTER 5

It is necessary for the soul to journey to God through this dark night.

1. There is a great distance between all that created things are in themselves and what God is in himself. Souls that spend their passions on any created thing are at as great a distance from God as created things are. Realizing this distance, Augustine records his conversation with God: Miserable man that I am, when will my littleness and imperfection be able to have fellowship with your uprightness? You indeed are good, and I am evil; you are merciful, and I am wicked; you are holy, I am miserable; you are just, I am unjust; you are light, I am blind; you, life, I, death; you, medicine, I, sickness; you, supreme truth, I, utter vanity.

2. The soul is ignorant to think it can reach union with God if it does not first empty itself of the desire for all things. There is enormous distance between transformation in God and our worldly state. When showing us this path, Jesus said: The one who refuses to renounce with the will all things he possesses cannot be my disciple. As long as the soul does not reject all things, it is incapable of receiving the Spirit of God in pure transformation.

3. If spiritual people only knew how much good they lose and what great fullness of spirit they lose when they do not raise their desires above childish things! If only they did not have the desire to taste worldly things, they would find the sweetness of all things in this simple spiritual food! But spiritual food gives them no pleasure for the same reason that the children of Israel did not taste the sweetness of all foods that the manna contained; they did not set apart their desire for it alone. They failed to find in the manna all the sweetness and strength that they could want, not because the manna did not contain these things, but because they desired something else. People who love some other thing together with God make little account of him, for they weigh in the balance against God that which is at the greatest possible distance from God. Since there is nothing that equals God, the soul that loves some other thing together with God does God a grievous wrong.

4. We can see this in God's command to Moses to ascend the mount to speak with him. God commanded Moses not only to ascend the mount alone, leaving the children of Israel below, but also not even to allow the beasts to feed near the mount. By this God signified that the soul that would ascend the mount of perfection in order to commune with God must not only renounce all things and leave them below, but must not even allow the desires, which are the beasts, to pasture near this mount. The faster a soul does this, the sooner it will reach the end of its journey. But until the desires are restrained the soul cannot reach the end, no matter how much it practices the virtues. The soul cannot

reach perfection in the virtues alone. Perfection comes from stripping and cleansing the soul of every desire.

5. Before ascending the mount, any soul that wants to ascend the mount to offer God the sacrifice of pure love and praise must do three things. First, it must cast away all foreign gods—that is, all passions and attachments foreign to God. Second, through the dark night of the senses it must purify itself of the remnants that the desires have left in the soul, by habitually denying them and relieving itself of them. Third, in order to reach this high mountaintop, it must have changed its garments.

6. If the soul successfully does the first two things, God will give the soul a new understanding of himself, casting the old human understanding aside. God will give the soul a new love for himself, the will being now stripped of all its old desires and human pleasures, and the soul being brought into a new state of knowledge and profound delight, casting away all other images and forms of knowledge. Everything that pertains to the old, natural self will be removed, and the soul will be clothed with a new supernatural aptitude with respect to all its faculties. Its operation, which before was human, will have become divine, attained in the state of union.

7. The soul becomes nothing other than an altar on which God is adored in praise and love, and God alone is on it. This is why God commanded that the altar on which the Ark of the Covenant was to be laid should be hollow inside: so that the soul may understand how completely empty God desires it to be in order to be an altar worthy of his majestic presence.

By this we should understand that love for God must never fail in the soul, so that the soul may be a worthy altar and so that no other love may be mingled with it.

8. God does not permit any other thing to dwell together with him. His will is that there should be only one desire where he is involved, which is to keep the law of God perfectly and to bear the cross of Christ. The soul that aspires to do nothing else other than keep the law of the Lord perfectly and bear the cross of Christ will be a true Ark, containing within itself the true manna, which is God.

CHAPTER 6
The desires cause two serious evils.

1. The desires cause two serious evils in the soul: They deprive the soul of the Spirit of God, and the soul in which they dwell is wearied, tormented, darkened, defiled, and weakened. Those two evils, the privative and the positive, can be caused by any disordered act of the desire. Speaking of the privative, the more the soul spends its passion on a created thing, the more the desire for that thing will fill the soul and the less capacity the soul will have for God.

2. The will cannot contain within itself both passion for created things and passion for God. What does the created thing have to do with the Creator? What does the sensual have to do with the spiritual? The visible with the invisible? The temporal with the eternal? Christlike poverty of spirit with attachment to anything in the world?

3.	As long as the soul is subjected to the sensual spirit, the pure and spiritual spirit cannot enter it. Jesus says not to take the children's bread and give it to the dogs. By these words our Lord compares those who renounce their creature-desires and prepare themselves to receive the Spirit of God in purity, to the children of God, and those who would have their desires feed on created things, to dogs.

4.	It is the nature of those who have desires always to be discontented and dissatisfied, like those who suffer hunger. What does the hunger that all created things suffer have to do with the fullness that the Spirit of God causes? This uncreated fullness cannot enter the soul if the soul does not first cast out the created hunger that pertains to the desires. Two opposite qualities—hunger and fullness—cannot exist in one soul.

5.	God's work in cleansing and purifying the soul is a greater work than creating the soul from nothing. These opposite desires oppose and resist God and God's Spirit.

6.	The desires are like restless, discontented children who are always demanding this or that from their mother and are never contented. Just as one who digs because he covets a treasure is wearied and fatigued, the soul is weary and fatigued in its quest to obtain what its desires demand of it. Although in the end the soul may obtain it, the soul is still weary because it is never satisfied; for the cisterns that it is digging are broken and cannot hold water to satisfy thirst.

7.	Desire is like a fire that increases as wood is thrown on it, and when it has consumed the wood, it dies. Actually, desire is worse: Fire goes down when the wood is consumed, but desire, though it increases when fuel is added to it, does not decrease in a corresponding way when the fuel is consumed. Instead of going down like the fire does when its fuel is consumed, it grows weak through weariness, for its hunger is increased and its food diminished.

CHAPTER 7
The desires torment the soul.

1. The desires also cause a second kind of positive evil in the soul by tormenting and afflicting it just as someone who is being tormented by being bound with cords has no relief until he is freed. Of these King David says: The cords of my sins, which are my desires, have constrained me all around.

2. The more intense the desire, the greater the torment it causes the soul. The torment increases with the desire, and the greater the desires that possess the soul, the greater its torments. Just as one who falls into his enemies' hands is tormented and afflicted, so is the soul that is led away by its desires. The book of Judges tells about Samson, the strong man who was once a judge of Israel. He fell into the power of his enemies, and they took his strength from him, put out his eyes, and bound him in a mill to grind corn, where they tormented and afflicted him greatly. So it happens in the soul in which its enemies, the desires, live and rule. The first thing they do is weaken the soul and blind it, and then they afflict and torment it, binding it to the mill of desire with the bonds of its own desire.

3. In his compassion God calls to those who are striving to free themselves from these bonds of desire. Through Jesus God offers refreshment for tormented and afflicted souls by saying: All you who go about tormented, afflicted, and burdened with the burden of your cares and desires, leave them, come to me, and I will refresh you, and you will find for your souls the rest that your desires—which are a heavy burden—take from you.

CHAPTER 8
The desires darken and blind the soul.

1. The third evil that the desires cause in the soul is that they blind and darken it. Even as clouds darken the sky and do not allow the bright sun to shine, or as a mirror that is clouded over cannot reflect a clear image, or as water defiled by mud does not reflect the face of one who looks into it, even so the soul that is clouded by the desires is darkened in its understanding, and allows neither the sun of natural reason nor that of the supernatural wisdom of God to illumine it clearly.

2. At the same time, when the soul is darkened in the understanding, it is made numb also in the will, and the memory becomes dull and disordered in its operation. As these faculties depend on the understanding, when the understanding is impeded they will become disordered and troubled.

3. Desire blinds and darkens the soul. In itself desire is blind, since it has no understanding in itself. Whenever the soul is

guided by desire, it becomes blind. As Jesus teaches: If the blind lead the blind, both fall into the pit. Desire does this to the soul, arousing its lust and dazzling its understanding so that it cannot see the light.

4. We can be saddened by the examples of those who burden themselves with extraordinary penitential practices, thinking that such rituals will bring them to union with the Divine. If these persons do not willingly restrain their desires, they will not achieve progress on the road to perfection and to the knowledge of God, and they will remain in darkness.

5. If people could only realize how great the blessing of divine light is and what great hurts and evils the desires make them fall into day after day! People must not rely on clear understanding or on gifts received from God, thinking that they can indulge their affection or desire and yet not be blinded and darkened. Gradually they fall into a worse condition.

6. Who would have said that one so perfect in wisdom and the gifts of God as was Solomon would have been reduced to such blindness and inertia of the will as to make altars to so many idols and to worship them himself when he was old? Yet no more was needed to bring him to this than the affection that he had for women and his neglect to deny the desires and delights of his heart. Solomon was so completely led away by his desires that they gradually blinded and darkened his understanding, so that in the end they succeeded in quenching the great light of wisdom God had given him.

7. If unrestrained desires could do so much in this man who knew so well the distance that lies between good and evil,

what might they accomplish in us who are not as wise as Solomon? At every step we hold evil to be good, and good, evil, and this arises from our own nature. As the prophet Isaiah tells us: We have groped for the wall as though we were blind, and we have been groping as though we had no eyes, and our blindness has reached such a point that we have stumbled at midday as though it were darkness. Those blinded by desire will not see what is good for them even if they are placed in the midst of the truth.

CHAPTER 9
The desires defile the soul.

1. The fourth evil that the desires cause in the soul is that they stain and defile it. There is more difference between excellence of soul and the best of created things than there is between pure diamond or fine gold, and tar. Just as gold or diamond, heated and placed on tar, would be stained by it, the soul that is hot with desire for any created thing draws forth impurity from it through the heat of its desire and is stained by it. Disordered desires defile the soul—the soul that is in itself a most lovely and perfect image of God.

2. Great harm is done to the beauty of the soul by its unruly desires for the things of this world. Although it is true that in its created being the soul is as perfect as when God created it, yet in its unruly being it is vile, abominable, and full of many evils. A single unruly desire is enough to bring a soul into such vileness that it cannot come into union

with God until the desire is purified. What, then, will be the vileness of the soul that is completely unrestrained with respect to its own passions and given up to its desires, and how far removed will it be from God and from his purity?

3. It is impossible to explain in words what impurity is caused in the soul by the various desires. If it could be expressed, it would be a thing of wonder, and it would fill us with pity to see how each desire, great or small, leaves in the soul its deposit of impurity and vileness, and how one single disorder of the reason can be the source of innumerable different impurities. The soul of the righteous person has one single perfection, which consists of uprightness of soul, innumerable gifts of the greatest richness, and many virtues of the greatest loveliness, each one different and full of grace according to the greatness of its love for God. In the same way the unruly soul, according to the variety of the desires that it has for created things, has within itself a miserable variety of impurities.

CHAPTER 10
The desires weaken the soul in virtue and make it lukewarm.

1. The fifth way in which the desires harm the soul is by making it lukewarm and weak so that it has no strength to follow after and practice virtue. The strength of the desires is diluted and weakened when it pursues various goals rather

than one single goal. If the desire of the will is dispersed among things other than virtue, it becomes weaker with regard to virtue. The soul that is not directed in one single desire for God loses warmth and vigor. King David understood this, for he said to God: I will keep my strength in you.

2. The desires bring no good to the soul but rather take from it what it possesses. If the soul does not restrain its desires, the desires grow so rapidly and to such an extent that they kill the soul with respect to God, because the soul has not first killed them. Then only the desires live in the soul.

3. Even if the desires do not reach this point in the soul, it is distressing to consider how the desires that live in the soul treat it, how unhappy the soul is with regard to itself, how dry with respect to its neighbors, and how weary and slothful with respect to the things of God. No evil mood can compare to the weariness and distaste for following virtue that the desire for created things gives to a soul. The reason many souls are not diligent in gaining virtue is that they have impure desires that are not fixed on God.

St. John is trying to say by good works "the seeker can be righteous

CHAPTER 11

p.39 *The soul that desires to reach divine union must be free from the slightest desire.*

1. The reader may wonder whether or not it is necessary to restrain all the desires, great and small, or if it is enough to restrain some of them and to leave others that do not seem

too harmful. It appears to be a severe and most difficult thing for the soul to be able to reach such purity and detachment from the world that it has no will or passion for anything.

2. First, it is true that all the desires are not equally hurtful, nor do they all discomfit the soul equally. The natural desires hinder the soul little, if at all, from reaching union. They do not hinder the soul in such a way as to prevent its union with the Divine. The natural person may well have natural desires, and yet the soul may be quite free from them. Sometimes the soul will be in the full union of quiet prayer at the time these desires are dwelling in the sensual part of the soul, and yet its higher part, which is in prayer, will have nothing to do with them.

3. But all the other voluntary desires must be driven away, every one, and the soul must be free from them all if it is to come to this complete union. The state of this divine union consists in the soul's total transformation in the will of God, so that there may be nothing in the soul that is contrary to God's will.

4. The state of divine union joins two wills into one: God's will is the soul's will. If the soul desired any imperfection that God did not will, there would not be one will of God since the soul would have a will for things for which God did not have a will. For the soul to come to unite itself perfectly with God through love and will, it must first be free from all desire of the will, however slight. It must not intentionally and knowingly consent with the will to imperfections, and it must have power and freedom to be

able not so to consent intentionally. The soul will eventually reach the stage of not even having these desires, for they develop out of a habit of imperfection.

5. For example, habitual imperfections are slight attachments—perhaps to a person or a book or a particular kind of food—that we never wish to conquer. Such imperfections do as much harm to the soul's growth and progress as any other imperfections that do not develop from habitual indulgence. As long as it has these attachments there is no possibility that it will make progress in perfection, even if the imperfection is extremely slight.

6. So the soul that is attached to anything, however much virtue it possesses, will not reach the freedom of divine union. It is sad to see certain souls in this plight. Like rich vessels, they are loaded with wealth, good works, spiritual practices, and the virtues and favors that God grants them. Yet, because they do not have the resolution to give up some whim, attachment, or passion, they never make progress or reach the port of perfection, though they would need to do no more than make one good passage to snap the cord of desire right off.

7. It is too bad that when God has given them strength to break other and stronger cords—that is, passions for sins and vanities—they fail to gain such a blessing because they have not shaken off some childish thing that God has asked them to conquer for love of him. Not only do they make no progress, but because of this attachment they fall back, lose what they have gained, and retrace that part of the road along which they have traveled at the cost of so much time

and labor. On this road, not to go forward is to turn back, and not to be gaining is to be losing. This Jesus taught us when he said: He that is not with me is against me; and he that does not gather with me scatters abroad. So one imperfection leads to another, and these lead to even more.

8. Many people to whom God has granted the favor of leading a long way into a state of great detachment from the world lose their spirituality and desire for God and holy solitude. Because they indulge in some slight attachment under the pretext of doing good or in the guise of conversation and friendship, they fall from the joy and wholehearted devotion that they had in their spiritual practices and eventually lose everything. All of this happens because they do not break with the beginnings of sensual desire and pleasure, and do not keep themselves in solitude for God.

9. We must continue along this road to reach our goal, but if our desires are not completely restrained, we will not reach complete divine union. The soul will not be transformed in God if it has even one imperfection. The soul has only one will, and if it is discomfited by anything and beset by anything, it is not free, solitary, and pure.

10. God deals a certain way with certain souls, taking them out of the world, taking away their sins, and destroying the occasions of sin that they encounter in the world so they can enter the Promised Land of divine union with greater freedom. Yet they harbor friendship for and make alliance with insignificant peoples, that is, with imperfections, and do not restrain them completely. Therefore Our

Lord is angry and allows them to fall into their desires and
to go from bad to worse.

11. If a person is to enter this divine union, all that lives in the
soul must die, both small and great, so that the soul must
be without desire for all this and detached from it. This Paul
teaches us clearly in his epistle to the Corinthians: This I
say to you, brothers, that the time is short; those who have
wives should be as if they had none, and those who weep
for the things of this world, as though they did not weep;
those who rejoice, as if they did not rejoice; those who buy,
as though they did not own; and those who use this world,
as if they did not. Paul says this to us in order to teach us
how completely our soul must be detached from all things
if it is to journey to God.

CHAPTER 12

The desires that suffice to cause
these evils in the soul.

1. We must now talk about how one embarks on this journey.

2. Is there any desire that is enough to produce in the soul
the evil that deprives the soul of God's grace and produces
the five serious harms of positive evil? Is there any desire,
however slight it is and of whatever kind, that is enough
to produce all these together? Or do some desires produce
some and others produce others? For example, do some
produce torment, while others produce weariness?

3. Privative evil, which consists in the soul's being deprived of God's grace, can be produced only by the voluntary desires. In this life they deprive the soul of grace, and in the next of glory, God's possession. Positive evils correspond to turning toward created things, even as the privative evils correspond to a turning away from God. The desire that most weakens grace will produce the most abundant torment, blindness, and defilement.

4. The reason any act of voluntary desire produces in the soul all these effects together lies in the direct opposition between them and all the acts of virtue that produce the opposite effects in the soul. Just as an act of virtue produces sweetness, peace, consolation, light, cleanness, and fortitude in the soul, an unruly desire causes torment, fatigue, weariness, blindness, and weakness. All the virtues grow through the practice of any one of them, and all the vices grow through the practice of any one of them, and the remnants of each grow in the soul.

5. The book that the angel commanded John to eat, in the book of Revelation, illustrates this well. The book was sweet to his mouth, but bitter in his belly. Desire, when it is carried into effect, is sweet and appears to be good, but it tastes bitter afterwards. The truth of this can be clearly proved by anyone who allows himself to be led away by it. Yet there are some persons so blind and insensible as not to feel this, for as they do not walk in God, they are unable to perceive what hinders them from approaching him.

6. I am not writing here of the other natural desires that are not voluntary, of thoughts that go not beyond their first

conceptions, or other temptations to which the soul does not consent. These produce in the soul none of the evils I have mentioned. Although one who suffers from them may think that the passion and disturbance they produce in him are defiling and blinding him, this is not the case. Instead, they are bringing him the opposite advantages. In so far as he resists them, he gains fortitude, purity, light, consolation, and many blessings, even as our Lord said to Paul: Strength is made perfect in weakness. But the voluntary desires produce all the evils mentioned before. Spiritual guides should restrain their disciples immediately with respect to any desire by causing them to remain without the objects of their desires, in order to free them from such great misery.

CHAPTER 13
The way that the soul must follow in order to enter this night of the senses.

1. In this section I must provide some information so the soul may know how to enter this night of the senses. We will explore the reasons this journey is called "night," and how many parts it has. The soul habitually enters this night of the senses in two ways: one active, the other passive. The active way consists in the things the soul can and does do by itself in order to enter the night of the senses. The passive way is one in which the soul does nothing, but God works in it, and it remains, so to speak, patient.

imitatio Christi
using "good works"

2. First, let the seeker have a habitual desire to imitate Christ in everything that he does, conforming himself to his life. Meditate on Christ's life in order to know how to imitate it, and behave in all things as Christ would behave.

3. Second, so that he can do this well, for the love of Jesus Christ he must renounce and completely reject every pleasure that is not purely for God's honor and glory. While Jesus was alive he desired no other pleasure than to do the will of his Father, which he called his meat and food. So if a person has the opportunity to listen to things that do not honor or serve God, he should not desire to listen to them. So it is with all the senses, insofar as he can fairly avoid the pleasure in question. If he cannot, it is enough that he wills not to take pleasure in this thing. In this way he will be able to restrain and empty the senses of such pleasure, as though they were in darkness. If he takes care to do this, he will soon reap great profit.

4. The following advice helps greatly in restraining the four natural passions, which are joy, hope, fear, and grief:

Strive always to prefer, not what is easiest, but what is most difficult;

Not what is most delectable, but what is most unpleasant;

Not what gives the most pleasure, but what gives the least;

Not what is restful, but what is wearisome;

Not what is consolation, but what is sorrow;

Not what is greatest, but what is least;

Not what is loftiest and most precious, but what is lowest and most despised;

Not what is a desire for anything, but what is a desire for
nothing.

Strive to go about seeking not the best of temporal things,
but the worst.

Strive so to desire to enter into complete detachment from
the world, and emptiness and poverty with respect to
everything that is in the world, for Christ's sake.

5. The soul should embrace these acts with all its heart and
strive to subdue its will. If it performs them with its heart,
it will quickly come to find in them great delight and
consolation, and to act with order and discretion.

6. If all these things are faithfully put into practice, they are
quite enough for entering into the night of the senses.
There is another kind of practice that teaches us to restrain
the lust of the flesh, the desire of the eyes, and the pride of
life, which are the things that reign in the world and from
which all the other desires proceed. Such a practice will
allow us to enter more completely into the night of the
senses:

7. First, let the soul strive to work on its own behalf, and
desire everyone to do so. Second, let it strive to speak
on its own behalf and desire everyone to do so. Third, let it
strive to think humbly of itself and desire everyone to do so.

8. It is helpful here to set down those lines that are written in
"The Ascent of the Mount," which is the poem at the beginning of this book. These lines are instructions for ascending
it, and so reaching the summit of union. Although it is true
that the words spoken there refer to the spiritual and interior,

they also refer to the spirit of imperfection according to sensual and exterior things. This can be seen by the two roads on either side of the path of perfection. We will understand them here as referring to the sensual. Afterward, in the second part of this night, they will be understood according to what is spiritual. The lines are these:

In order to arrive at having pleasure in everything,
Desire to have pleasure in nothing.
In order to arrive at possessing everything,
Desire to possess nothing.
In order to arrive at being everything,
Desire to be nothing.
In order to arrive at knowing everything,
Desire to know nothing.
In order to arrive at the place where you have no pleasure,
You must go by a way in which you have no pleasure.
In order to arrive at what you do not know,
You must go by a way that you do not know.
In order to arrive at what you do not possess,
You must go by a way that you do not possess.
In order to arrive at what you are not,
You must go through what you are not.
When your mind dwells on anything,
You are ceasing to cast yourself on the All.
For, in order to pass from the all to the All,
You have to deny yourself wholly in all.
And when you come to possess it wholly,
You must possess it without desiring anything.

For if you will have anything in having all,
You do not have your treasure purely in God.

9.   In this detachment from the world the spiritual soul finds its
quiet and repose. Since it desires nothing, nothing wearies it
when it is lifted up and nothing oppresses it when it is cast
down, because it is in the center of its humility. But the
moment it desires anything, it becomes wearied.

CHAPTER 14

The second phrase of the stanza is explained:

"aroused in love with yearnings."

1.   We have explained the first phrase of this stanza, which
describes the night of the senses, telling what this night of
the senses is and why it is called night. We have also described
the order and manner that the soul should follow actively to
enter this night. I want to describe now the properties and
effects of this night, for they are wonderful.

2.   The soul says that "aroused in love with yearnings," it passed
through this dark night of the senses and came to the union
of the Beloved. In order to conquer all the desires and to deny
itself the pleasures that it has in everything, and for which its
love arouses the will so that it may enjoy them, it would need
to experience another and a greater arousal by another and a
better love, which is that of its Bridegroom. Setting its pleasure
on him and deriving its strength from him, the soul should

have courage and constancy easily to deny itself all other things. In order to conquer the strength of the desires of the senses, it would need not only to have love for its Bridegroom, but also to be aroused by love and to have longings.

3.   With such longings of desire the sensual nature is attracted to sensual things. But if the spiritual part is not aroused with other and greater longings for spiritual things, it will be unable to throw off the yoke of nature or to enter this night of the senses. Nor will it have courage to remain in darkness as to all things, depriving itself of desire for them all.

4.   It is impossible to describe the nature and all the varieties of these longings of love that souls experience in the early stages of the road to union. Nor is it possible to describe the diligent means and devices that they use to leave behind their house, which is self-will, during the night of the restraining of their senses. It is even impossible to describe how easy, and even sweet and delectable, these longings for the Bridegroom make all the trials and perils of this night to appear to them.

CHAPTER 15

The remainder of the first stanza is explained:

". . . oh, happy chance!—I went forth without being observed, since all in my house were asleep."

1.   These lines take as a metaphor the miserable state of captivity. When one is held captive but none of the jailers hinders his release, he considers this a "happy chance." Because of

original sin the soul is so to speak a captive in this mortal body, subject to the passions and desires of nature. The soul considers it a "happy chance" that it is able to go forth from its slavery to its natural passions without being hindered by any of them.

2. To this end the soul profited by going forth on a "dark night"—that is, in depriving itself of every pleasure and restraining every desire. Its "house being now at rest" refers to the sensual desires of the soul, which are now at rest because the soul has overcome them and lulled them to sleep. The soul does not go forth to true freedom and union with its Beloved until its desires are lulled to sleep through the denial of the sensual nature.

BOOK TWO

The second part of this night pertains to the spirit.

The second stanza is introduced:

"In darkness and secure, by the secret ladder,
disguised—oh, happy chance!—
In darkness and in concealment, my house
being now at rest."

1. In the second stanza the soul sings of the happy fortune it experienced in stripping the spirit of all spiritual imperfections and desires for the possession of spiritual things. This was a much greater happiness. There is greater difficulty in putting to rest the spiritual part by entering this interior darkness, which is spiritual detachment from all things sensual or spiritual, and leaning on pure faith alone and an ascent to God.

2. The soul here calls this "a ladder," and "secret," because all its rungs and parts are secret and hidden from all sense and

understanding. So the soul has remained in darkness as to all light of sense and understanding, going forth beyond all limits of nature and reason in order to ascend by this divine ladder of faith, which reaches and penetrates even to the heights of God.

3.   The soul says that it was traveling "disguised" because the clothes it wears and its natural condition are changed into divine ones as it ascends by faith. Because of this disguise it was recognized or hindered neither by time nor by reason nor by the devil. None of these things can harm one who journeys in faith. The soul travels so well concealed and hidden and is so far from all the deceits of the devil that it truly journeys "in darkness and in concealment"—that is, hidden from the devil, to whom the light of faith is more than darkness.

4.   The soul that journeys through this night journeys in concealment and in hiding from the devil. So the soul says that it went forth securely "in darkness." One who takes faith as guide and leaves behind all natural imaginings and spiritual reasoning journeys securely. Therefore when the soul reaches the union that is of God, its natural faculties are at rest, as are the longings of its senses in its spiritual part.

5.   Because of this the soul does not say here that it went forth with longings, as in the first night of the senses. To journey in the night of the senses and to strip itself of things related to the senses, it needed longings of love so that it might go forth perfectly. But to put to rest the house of its spirit, the soul needs no more than denial of all faculties and pleasures

and desires of the spirit in pure faith. This achieved, the soul is united with the Beloved in a union of simplicity, purity, and love.

6.   We must remember that when speaking of the senses the first stanza says that the soul went forth on "a dark night." Here, speaking of the spirit, it says that it went forth "in darkness." The darkness of the spirit is by far the greater, even as complete and true darkness is always greater than night. However dark a night may be, something can always be seen. But in true darkness nothing can be seen. In the night of the senses there still remains some light, for the understanding and reason remain and are not blinded. This spiritual night, which is faith, deprives the soul of everything, both as to understanding and as to sense. That is why the soul in this night says that it was journeying "in darkness and secure." The less the soul works with its own ability, the more securely it journeys, because it journeys more in faith.

CHAPTER 2
The second cause of this night of faith.

1.   The second part of this night, which is faith, is the wondrous means that leads to the goal: God, who is also the third part of the soul's night. Faith, which is the means, is compared with midnight. We can say that it is darker for the soul than either the first part or the third.

2. The first part, the dark night of the senses, is comparable to the beginning of night, or the time when tangible objects can no longer be seen. This part of night is not as far removed from light as midnight is. The third part, the period preceding the dawn, is quite close to the light of day, and therefore it too is not as dark as midnight is. It is now close to the enlightenment and illumination of the light of day, which is compared with God.

3. Although God is as dark a night to the soul as is faith, when these three parts of the night are over God enlightens the soul with the rays of his divine light. This is the beginning of the perfect union that follows when the third night is past.

CHAPTER 3
Faith is dark night to the soul.

1. Faith, the theologians say, is a habit of the soul, certain and obscure. The reason it is an obscure habit is that it makes us believe truths revealed by God himself that transcend all natural light and exceed all human understanding. For the soul this excessive light of faith that is given to it is thick darkness; it overwhelms greater things and does away with small things, even as the light of the sun overwhelms all other lights. When it shines and disables our visual faculty, other lights do not appear to be lights at all. Even so the light of faith, by its excessive greatness, suppresses and disables the light of the understanding.

2. People can know nothing by themselves except what they learn through their senses. Because of this the forms of objects must be already present in the soul. From the object that is present, knowledge is born in the soul. If one spoke to someone about things he has never been able to understand and whose images he has never seen, he would not be enlightened about them. If you say to someone that on a certain island there is an animal that he has never seen, and give no idea of that animal's image so he can compare it with others that he has seen, he will not know any more about it than he did before, no matter how hard you try to describe it.

3. It is like this with faith as it applies to the soul. Faith tells us of things we have never seen or understood. We have never seen or understood anything that resembles them, since there is nothing that resembles them at all. We have no light of natural knowledge about them, since what we are told about these things bears no relation to any of our senses. We know it by the ear alone, believing what we are taught, bringing our natural light into subjection, and treating it as if it did not exist. As Paul says: Faith is not knowledge that enters by any of the senses, but is only the consent given by the soul to what enters through the ear.

4. Faith far transcends even these qualities. Not only does it provide no knowledge, but also it deprives us of all other information and knowledge and blinds us to them, so that they cannot judge it well. Other knowledge can be acquired by the light of the understanding, but the knowledge that comes from faith is acquired without the enlightenment

of the understanding, which is rejected for faith. So Isaiah said: If you do not believe, you will not understand. It is clear, then, that faith is dark night for the soul, and it is in this way that it gives it light. The more the soul is darkened, the greater is the light that comes to it.

5. So faith, because it is dark night, gives light to the soul, which is in darkness. In the delights of my pure contemplation and union with God, the night of faith will be my guide. The soul must be in darkness in order to have light for this road.

CHAPTER 4

The soul must also be in darkness with respect to spiritual things.

1. In order to be effectively guided to this state by faith, the soul must not only be in darkness with respect to the sensual and lower part, but it must also be blinded and darkened with respect to the higher and rational part that has to do with spiritual things. For someone to reach supernatural transformation, that person must be plunged into darkness and carried far away from all that is sensual and rational in his nature.

2. Although this transformation and union is something that cannot be comprehended by human ability and the senses, the soul must completely and voluntarily empty itself of all that can enter into it. Who will prevent God from doing whatever he wants to do in the soul that is resigned, reduced to nothing, and detached?

3. If a person is not quite blind, that person often refuses to be led by a guide. Since he sees a little, he thinks it is best to go in whatever direction he can distinguish because he sees no better direction. So he can lead astray a guide who sees more than he, for after all, he tells the guide where to go. Also a soul may lean on any knowledge or feeling of its own. However great this knowledge might be, it is small and far different from what God is. A soul must pass beyond everything to unknowing.

4. Passing beyond all that can be known and understood, both spiritually and naturally, the soul will desire with all its heart to come to what in this life cannot be known. Leaving behind all that it experiences and feels, both temporally and spiritually, and all that it is able to experience and feel in this life, it will desire with all its heart to come to what surpasses all feeling and experience. In order to be free to do this, it must not hold onto anything it receives within itself, either spiritually or sensually, considering it all to be of much less account.

5. The more emphasis the soul lays on what it understands, experiences, and imagines, and the more it esteems this, the more it loses of the supreme good, and the more it is hindered from attaining the supreme good. The less it thinks of what it may have and the more it dwells on the highest good, the closer it will get to this higher good.

CHAPTER 5

What is meant by "union of the soul with God."

1. To understand what this divine union means we must understand that God dwells and is present substantially in every soul, even in the soul of the greatest sinner in the world. God continually works this kind of union between God and all created things, for in it he is preserving their being.

2. Union of the soul with God is attained when the likeness that comes from love is produced. We will therefore call this the union of likeness, even as that other union is called substantial or essential. The former is natural, the latter supernatural. The latter happens when the two wills—that of the soul and that of God—are conformed together in one, and there is nothing in the one that repels the other. When the soul rids itself totally of what is repelled by the divine will, refusing to conform to it, it is transformed in God through love.

3. Although it is true that God is always in the soul, creating and sustaining its natural being, he does not always communicate supernatural being to it. This is communicated only by love and grace, which not all souls possess. God communicates himself most to the soul that has progressed farthest in love, meaning that its will is in closest conformity with the will of God.

4. It is this that John wanted to explain when he said: He gave power to be sons of God—that is, to be transformed in God—only to those who are born, not of blood—that

is, not of natural constitution and temperament—neither of the will of the flesh—that is, of the free will of natural capacity and ability—still less of the will of man—in which is included every manner of judging and comprehending with the understanding. He gave power to none of these to become sons of God, but only to those that are born of God—that is, to those who, being born again through grace and dying first of all to everything that is of the old nature, are raised above themselves to the supernatural and receive from God this rebirth and adoption that transcends all that can be imagined. As John says elsewhere: One who is not born again in the Holy Spirit will not be able to see the kingdom of God, which is the state of perfection. To be born again in the Holy Spirit in this life is to have a soul like God in purity, having in itself no imperfection.

5.   In allowing God to work in it, the soul is at once illumined and transformed in God, and God communicates to it his supernatural being in such a way that it looks like God himself and has all that God himself has. This union occurs when God grants the soul this supernatural favor, that all the things of God and the soul are one.

6.   The soul's preparation for this union is not that it should understand or perceive or feel or imagine anything concerning either God or anything else, but that it should have purity and love—that is, perfect resignation and detachment from everything for God's sake alone. Since there can be no perfect transformation if there is not perfect purity, and as the enlightenment, illumination, and union of the soul with God will be according to the

proportion of its purity, the soul will not be perfect if it is not perfectly clean.

7.   A soul according to its capacity may have reached union, yet not all do so in an equal degree. This depends on what the Lord is pleased to grant to each one. This is how souls see God in heaven. Some see more, some less; but all see him, and all are content, for their capacity is satisfied. Although in our earthly life we find certain souls enjoying equal peace and tranquility in the state of perfection, each one of them satisfied, some of them may be many degrees higher than others. All, however, will be equally satisfied, because the capacity of each one is satisfied.

CHAPTER 6
The three theological virtues perfect the three faculties of the soul.

1.   The three theological virtues—faith, hope, and charity, which have respect to the faculties of understanding, memory, and will as their proper supernatural objects, and by means of which the soul is united with God according to its faculties, produce the same emptiness and darkness, each one in its own faculty: faith, in the understanding; hope, in the memory; and charity, in the will.

2.   These three virtues cause emptiness in the faculties: Faith, in the understanding, causes an emptiness and darkness with respect to understanding; hope, in the memory, causes

emptiness of all possessions; and charity causes emptiness in the will, and detachment from all affection and from rejoicing in all that is not God. Faith tells us what cannot be understood with the understanding. Paul spoke of it in Hebrews: We interpret faith as the substance of things hoped for. Faith, although it brings certainty to the understanding, brings to it not clearness, but obscurity.

3. As to hope, there is no doubt that it renders the memory empty and dark with respect both to things below and to things above. Hope always relates to what is not possessed; for if it were possessed, there would be no more hope. This virtue also produces emptiness, for it has to do with what is not possessed and not with what is possessed.

4. Charity causes emptiness in the will with respect to all things, since it obliges us to love God above them all. This cannot be unless we withdraw our affection from them in order to set it wholly on God. So all these three virtues set the soul in obscurity and emptiness with respect to all things.

5. Here we must consider the parable that our Redeemer related in the eleventh chapter of Luke, telling the story of a man who had to go out at midnight in order to ask his friend for three loaves of bread; the loaves signify these three virtues. He said that the man asked for them at midnight in order to show that the soul that is in darkness as to all things must acquire these three virtues according to its faculties and must perfect itself in them in this night.

6. To these three virtues, then, we have to lead the three faculties of the soul, informing each faculty by each one of them and stripping it and setting it in darkness concerning

all things except for these three virtues. This is the spiritual night that just now we called active; for the soul does what lies within its ability in order to enter into it.

7.   In this method all security is found against the wiles of the devil and against the effectiveness of self-love and its ramifications. Self-love desires most subtly to deceive and hinder spiritual persons on their road when they do not know how to become detached and to govern themselves according to these virtues. So they are never able to reach the substance and purity of spiritual good, nor do they journey by as straight and short a road as they might.

CHAPTER 7
The way that leads to eternal life is narrow.

1.   We now have to describe the detachment from the world and the purity of the three faculties of the soul. To this end we must carefully note the words that Our Savior used in the seventh chapter of Matthew concerning this road: How narrow is the gate and how narrow the way that leads unto life, and few there are that find it! It is as if he had said: In truth the way is narrow, more so than you think. We must note that he says first that the gate is narrow, to make it clear that in order for the soul to enter by this gate, which is Christ, and which comes at the beginning of the road, the will must first be narrowed and detached from all things sensual and temporal, and it must love God above them all. All this pertains to the night of the senses.

2. He then says that the way is narrow—that is to say, the way of perfection—in order to make it clear that to travel on the way of perfection, the soul not only has to enter by the narrow gate, emptying itself of things of the senses, but also has to restrict itself, freeing and disencumbering itself completely of what pertains to the spirit. So we can apply what he says of the narrow gate to the sensual part of man; and what he says of the narrow road we can apply to the spiritual or the rational part. And when he says: There are few who find it, we must note the reason for this, which is that there are few who are able to enter, and also desire to enter, into this complete detachment from the world and emptiness of spirit.

3. Not only must the soul be disencumbered from what pertains to created things, but also, as it travels, it must be reduced to nothing and detached from all that pertains to its spirit. Therefore Our Lord said this: If anyone will follow my road, let him deny himself and take up his cross and follow me. Anyone who desires to save his soul will lose it; but anyone who loses it for my sake, will gain it.

4. Oh, that someone could show us how to understand, practice, and experience what this counsel is that our Savior gives us here concerning self-denial, so that spiritual persons might see in how different a way they should conduct themselves on this road from the way many of them think proper! True spirituality seeks for God's sake what is distasteful rather than what is delectable, and it inclines itself rather to suffering than to consolation.

5.   Oh, that someone could tell us how far Our Lord desires this self-denial to be carried! It must certainly be like death and annihilation, temporal, natural, and spiritual, in all things that the will esteems, in which consists all self-denial.

6.   This is what Our Lord meant when he said: He who would save his life shall lose it. That is, one who will possess anything or seek anything for himself shall lose it, and one who loses his soul for my sake will gain it. In other words, one who for Christ's sake renounces all that his will can desire and enjoy, and chooses what is most like the Cross, shall gain it. When two disciples begged Our Lord for a place on his right hand and on his left, he offered them instead the chalice that he had to drink as a thing more precious and more secure on this earth than is the possession of pleasurable things.

7.   This chalice is death to the natural self, a death attained through detaching oneself from the world and bringing that self to nothing, in order that the soul may travel by this narrow path with respect to all its connections with the senses and to the spirit. On this way there is room only for self-denial and the Cross. Therefore Our Lord said through Matthew: My yoke is easy and my burden is light. And this burden is the cross.

8.   The soul that practices this suffering and being brought to nothing will achieve all that other practices can achieve, and even more. For progress does not come except through following the example of Christ, who is the Way, the Truth, and the Life, and no one comes to the Father but by him. So any spirituality that desires to walk in sweetness and

with ease and flees from following Christ's example, is worthless.

9. I will now explain how we are to die, following the example of Christ, for he is our example and light. In the first place he died as to the senses, spiritually, in his life, besides dying naturally at his death.

10. In the second place, at the moment of his death he was also reduced to nothing in his soul and was deprived of any relief and consolation, since his Father had left him in the most intense dryness of soul. Therefore he was forced to cry out: My God! My God! Why hast thou forsaken me? This was the greatest desolation, with respect to the senses, that he had suffered in his life. Thus he accomplished the greatest work that he had ever done, whether in miracles or in mighty works, during the whole of his life: the reconciliation and union of mankind, through grace, with God.

11. This was the moment when Our Lord was most completely reduced to nothing in everything. He was reduced to nothing with respect to human reputation, for when men saw him die, they mocked him rather than esteemed him. He was also reduced to nothing with respect to nature, since his nature was reduced to nothing when he died. Further, he was reduced to nothing with respect to the spiritual consolation and protection of the Father, since at that time the Father forsook him, so that he might pay the whole debt of mankind and unite us with God by being reduced to nothing.

12. In the same way, when at last the spiritual person is reduced to nothing, which will be the greatest extreme of humility,

spiritual union will be brought about between the soul and God. This does not consist in refreshment and in consolations and spiritual feelings, but in a living death of the Cross, both as to sense and as to spirit—that is, both inwardly and outwardly.

CHAPTER 8

Faith is the means by which the soul may attain to the divine union of love.

1. For the understanding to be prepared for divine union, it must be pure and empty of all that pertains to the senses and detached from all that the understanding can grasp. This we learn from an illustration in the Holy Scriptures. When Solomon had completed the building of the temple, God came down in darkness and filled the temple so that the children of Israel could not see. Then Solomon said: The Lord has promised that he will dwell in darkness.

2. God also appeared in darkness to Moses on the Mount, where God was concealed. Whenever God communicated himself intimately, he appeared in darkness.

3. We have a good illustration of this in the story of Gideon's army: All his soldiers had lamps in their hands, but no one could not see them because the lamps were concealed in the darkness of the pitchers. When the soldiers broke the pitchers the light could be seen. The same thing happens with faith, which is foreshadowed by those pitchers. Within

itself faith contains divine light. When faith is ended and broken at the ending and breaking of this mortal life, the glory and light of the Divinity that was contained in it will appear, and it will see God face to face in glory.

CHAPTER 9

Harm results from the soul not being able to detach itself from natural things of the mind.

1. We must now turn to the interior physical senses—that is, the imagination and the fancy. These we must also empty of all the imaginary things and forms that may pertain to them by nature, and we must prove how impossible it is for the soul to reach union with God until their operation ceases in it, since they cannot be the proper and direct means of this union.

2. The senses of which we are here particularly speaking are the two interior physical senses called imagination and fancy, which work closely together. All the things that these senses can receive and fashion are known as imaginations and fancies, which are forms presented to the senses by physical figures and images.

3. This can happen in two ways. One way is supernatural, in which representation can be made to these senses passively, without any effort of their own. These we call "visions that take place in the mind," produced after a supernatural manner. The other way is natural, in which, through the

ability of the soul, these things can be actively fashioned in it through forms, figures, and images.

4. All these imaginings must be cast out from the soul, which must then remain in darkness as far as this sense is concerned, so that it may reach divine union. For these mental imaginings can bear no proportion to direct means of union with God, any more than can the physical imaginings, which serve as objects to the five exterior senses.

5. The reason for this is that the imagination cannot fashion or imagine anything at all beyond what it has experienced through its exterior senses—that is, what it has seen with the eyes, or heard with the ears, and so on. At most it can only compose likenesses of the things that it has seen or heard or felt, which are of no more consequence than those that the previously mentioned senses have received, nor are they even of as much consequence.

6. Therefore those who imagine God using any of these figures, or as a great fire or brightness or any other such form, and think that anything of this sort will be like him, are far from approaching him. These considerations and forms and manners of meditation are necessary to beginners so that they may gradually feed and enkindle their souls with love by means of the senses. Although they serve as remote means to union with God, through which souls commonly have to pass in order to reach the goal and abode of spiritual repose, yet they must merely pass through them. They must not remain forever in them, for in such a manner they would never reach their goal, which neither resembles these remote means nor has anything to do with them.

7. Whether beginners or ones more advanced, all must learn to abide attentively and wait lovingly on God in a state of quiet, and to devote no attention either to imagination or to its working. For here the faculties are at rest, and are working—not actively, but passively—by receiving what God works in them.

CHAPTER 10
The soul must be emptied of things of the senses.

1. The progressing spiritual person who desires to enter on the spiritual road (which is that of contemplation) must leave the way of imagination and of meditation through the senses when he no longer takes pleasure in it and is unable to reason. There are two reasons for this. The first is that in one way the soul has received all the spiritual good that it can derive from the things of God by the path of meditation and reasoning. The sign that this is so is that it can no longer meditate or reason as before, and finds no new sweetness or pleasure in meditation as it found before.

2. The second reason is that the soul at this point now has both the substance and the habit of the spirit of meditation. The goal of reasoning and meditation on the things of God is gaining some knowledge and love of God. Each time that the soul gains this through meditation, there is an action. And just as many actions, of whatever kind, end by forming a habit in the soul, many of these actions of loving knowledge that the soul has been making one after

another from time to time come through repetition to be so continuous in it that they become habitual.

3. God wants souls to achieve this end without the intervention of actions by setting them at once in contemplation. So what previously the soul was gaining gradually through its labor of meditation on particular facts has now through practice changed into a habit of loving knowledge, of a general kind, and not distinct as before.

4. Therefore, when the soul gives itself to prayer it is now like one to whom water has been brought, so that he drinks peacefully, without labor, and is no longer forced to draw the water through the aqueducts of past meditations and forms and figures. Then, as soon as the soul comes before God, it makes an act of knowledge, loving, passive, and tranquil, in which it drinks of wisdom and love and delight.

5. The soul will frequently find itself in this loving or peaceful state of waiting on God without in any way exercising its faculties and without working actively at all, but only receiving. In order to reach this state, it will frequently need to make use of meditation, quietly and in moderation. But when once the soul is brought into this other state, it does not act at all with its faculties.

6. When the soul has completely purified and emptied itself of all tangible forms and images, it will remain in pure and simple light, being transformed in it into a state of perfection. If all impediments were removed, the soul would then find itself in a condition of pure detachment from the world and poverty of spirit, and, being simple and pure, would be transformed into simple and pure Wisdom, which is

the Son of God. When the enamored soul finds that the natural has failed it, it is then imbued with the Divine, both naturally and supernaturally, so that there may be no vacuum in its nature.

7. When the spiritual person cannot meditate, let him learn to be still in God, fixing his loving attention on him in the calm of his understanding, although he may think himself to be doing nothing. Little by little, divine calm and peace will be infused into his soul, together with a wondrous knowledge of God, enfolded in divine love.

CHAPTER 11
The soul must not lean on visions that take place in the mind.

1. We will now turn to supernatural things. These are called "visions that take place in the mind." These also pertain to the senses, since they come within the category of images, forms, and figures, exactly as do the natural things.

2. It must be understood that under this term "vision that takes place in the mind" we include all things that can be presented to the mind supernaturally by means of any image, form, figure, and species. All that through the five physical senses is presented to the soul and dwells within it in a natural manner may also occur in the soul in a supernatural manner, without any assistance of the outward senses. The sense of visualization, together with

memory, is an archive and storehouse of the understanding, in which are received all forms and images that can be understood. The soul has them within itself as if in a mirror, having received them either by means of the five senses or supernaturally. It presents them to the understanding, after which the understanding considers them and judges them. Not only so, but also the soul can prepare and visualize others like those with which it is acquainted.

3. Even as the five outward senses present the images of their objects to the inward senses, so, supernaturally, without using the outward senses, both God and the devil can present the same images and much more beautiful and perfect ones. Beneath these images God often presents many things to the soul and teaches it much wisdom.

4. This we continually see in the Holy Scriptures, as when Isaiah saw God in his glory behind the smoke that covered the Temple, and behind the seraphim who covered their faces and their feet with wings, and as Jeremiah saw the rod watching, and as Daniel saw a multitude of visions.

5. The devil, too, strives to deceive the soul with his visions, which in appearance are good. This can be seen in the Book of Kings, when he deceived all the prophets of Ahab, presenting to their minds the horns with which he said the king was to destroy the Assyrians, which was a lie. Such also were the visions of Pilate's wife, warning him not to condemn Christ.

6. There are many other places where we see how, in this mirror of the mind, visions that take place in the mind come more frequently to proficient souls than do outward

and physical visions. These are no different from those that enter by the outward senses, except in the effect that they produce. In the degree of their perfection there is a great difference, for visions that take place in the mind are subtler and produce a deeper impression on the soul, inasmuch as they are supernatural and are more interior than exterior supernatural visions.

7.   It is to these senses of visualization and imagination that the devil habitually presents himself with his wiles—sometimes natural, sometimes supernatural. For they are the door and entrance to the soul, and here the understanding comes to take up or set down its goods, as if it were in a harbor or in a storehouse where it keeps its provisions. It is here that both God and the devil always come with their jewels of supernatural forms and images, to offer them to the understanding. God, however, does not make use of this means alone to instruct the soul, but dwells within it in substance.

8.   With regard to all these visions that take place in the mind, and to all other forms that present themselves under some particular kind of image or form, whether they are false and come from the devil or are recognized as true and coming from God, the understanding must neither be discomfited by them nor feed on them. Neither must the soul desire to receive them or to have them, thereby the soul runs the risk of being no longer detached, free, pure, and simple, without any mode or manner, as is required for union.

9.   That there is no form or likeness in God is clearly declared by the Holy Spirit in Deuteronomy, which says: You heard

the voice of God's words, and you saw in him no form whatsoever. But there was darkness there, and clouds and thick darkness, which are the confused and dark knowledge in which the soul is united with God.

10. Therefore, in order to come to this essential union of love in God, the soul must take care not to lean on visions that take place in the mind, or on forms or figures or particular objects of the understanding. These cannot serve it as a proper means to such an end. Rather, they perturb it, and for this reason the soul must renounce them and strive not to have them. The visions that take place in the mind, like the outward physical visions of which we have spoken, do the soul good by communicating to it intelligence or love or sweetness. But for them to produce this effect in the soul it is not necessary for the soul to desire to receive them.

11. When the soul completely detaches itself in its will from grasping at the forms, images, and figures of the spiritual communications that we have described, not only is it not deprived of the communications and the blessings that they cause within it, but it is much better prepared to receive them with greater abundance, clearness, freedom of spirit, and simplicity when all these things are set to one side.

12. Therefore the eyes of the soul must always be withdrawn from all things that it can see and understand distinctly, which are communicated through the senses. These do not make for a foundation of faith or for reliance on faith, so the soul must be set on what it does not see: things that pertain not to the senses but to the spirit—which cannot be expressed by any figure of the senses.

CHAPTER 12
Why God allows supernatural visions.

1. Since in these supernatural visions there is so much hindrance and peril to progress, why does God, who is most wise and desires to remove stumbling blocks and snares from the soul, offer and communicate them to it?

2. In order to answer this, it is good first of all to set down three fundamental points. The first is from Paul to the Romans, where he says: The works that are done are ordained of God. The second is from the Holy Spirit in the Book of Wisdom, where he says: The wisdom of God, although it extends from one end to another—that is to say, from one extreme to another—orders all things with sweetness. The third is from the theologians, who say that God moves all things according to their nature.

3. If God is to move the soul and to raise it up from the extreme depth of its lowliness to the extreme height of his loftiness, in divine union with himself, he must do so with order and sweetness and according to the nature of the soul itself. Then, since the order by which the soul acquires knowledge is through forms and images of created things, and the natural way in which it acquires this knowledge is through the senses, it follows that if God is to raise up the soul to supreme knowledge and to do so with sweetness, he must begin to work from the lowest and extreme end of the senses of the soul. This he must do in order to gradually lead it, according to its own nature, to the other extreme of his spiritual wisdom, which does not pertain to the senses.

Therefore he first leads it onward by instructing it through forms, images, and ways of the senses, according to its own method of understanding, sometimes naturally, sometimes supernaturally, and by means of reasoning, to this supreme Spirit of God.

4. Therefore the mature spirit devotes no attention to the senses, nor does it receive anything through the senses or make any great use of them. It does not need to do so in its relations with God, as it did previously when it had not grown spiritually. This is the meaning of the passage from Paul's letter to the Corinthians that says: When I was a child, I spoke as a child, I knew as a child, I thought as a child; but when I became a man, I put away childish things.

CHAPTER 13
Spiritual teachers may lead disciples into error.

1. The reason that has now moved me to write at length about this is the lack of discretion that I have observed in certain spiritual teachers. Trusting in supernatural things and believing that they are good and come from God, both teachers and disciples have fallen into great error and have found themselves in dire straits. This fulfills Our Savior's saying: If the blind lead the blind, both fall into the pit. He does not say "will fall," but "fall."

2. If the spiritual director has an inclination toward revelations of such a kind that they mean something to him, or satisfy or delight his soul, it is impossible for him not to impress

that delight and that aim on the spirit of his disciple, even without realizing it, unless the disciple is more advanced than he. From his inclination toward such visions and the pleasure that he takes in them, he develops a certain kind of esteem for them. Unless he watches this esteem carefully, he cannot fail to communicate some indication of it to other persons. If that person is like-minded and has a similar inclination, it is impossible for there not to be communicated from one to the other a readiness to grasp these things and hold them in great esteem.

3. In this lies a great delusion, for revelations or locutions that are of God do not always turn out as people expect or as they imagine inwardly. One must never believe or trust them blindly, even though they are known to be revelations or answers or sayings of God.

CHAPTER 14
We may be deceived about visions and locutions that come from God.

1. Although visions and locutions that come from God are true and in themselves are always certain, they are not always so with respect to ourselves. One reason is the defective way in which we understand them, and the other, the variety of their causes. They are not always as they seem, nor do they turn out as they appear to our manner of thinking.

2. The reason for this is that since God is vast and boundless, he desires in his prophecies, locutions, and revelations to

employ methods of seeing things that differ greatly from such purpose and method as we can normally understand. These are the truer and the more certain, the less they seem so to us. This we constantly see in the Holy Scriptures. To many of the ancients, a number of God's prophecies and locutions did not come to pass as they expected because they understood them after their own manner, in the wrong way, and quite literally.

3. In Genesis, God said to Abraham, when he had brought him to the land of the Canaanites: I will give you this land. When God had said this to him many times, and Abraham was by now old, and God had never given it to him, Abraham asked God once again: Lord, by what sign am I to know that I am to possess it? Then God revealed to him that he was not to possess it in person, but that his descendants would do so after four hundred years. Then Abraham understood the promise, which in itself was most true, for in giving it to his descendants for love of him, God was giving it to Abraham himself.

4. And so Abraham was deceived by the way in which he himself had understood the prophecy. If he had then acted according to his own understanding of it, those who saw him die without its having been given to him might have erred greatly, for they were not to see the time of its fulfillment. And as they had heard him say that God would give it to him, they would have been confused and would have believed it to be false.

5. God also appeared to Abraham's grandson, Jacob, when Jacob's son Joseph brought him to Egypt because of the

famine in Canaan. When he was on the road, God appeared and said: Jacob, do not be afraid; go down into Egypt, and I will go down there with you. And when you go forth again from there, I will bring you out and guide you. This promise, as it would seem according to our own manner of understanding, was not fulfilled, for Jacob died in Egypt and never left it alive.

6. The word of God was to be fulfilled in Jacob's descendants, whom God brought out from Egypt after many years, being himself their guide on the way. Anyone who had known of this promise that God made to Jacob would have considered it certain that Jacob, even as he had gone to Egypt alive by the command and favor of God, would most certainly leave it, alive and in his own person, in the same form and manner as he went there, since God had promised him a favorable return. Such a one would have been deceived and would have marveled greatly when he saw Jacob die in Egypt, and the promise, in the sense in which he understood it, remained unfulfilled. So, while the words of God are in themselves most true, it is possible to be greatly mistaken with regard to them.

7. Souls are often deceived with respect to revelations that come from God, because they interpret them according to their apparent sense and literally, whereas God's principal intention in giving these things is to convey the spirit contained in them, which is difficult to understand. The spirit is much more charged with meaning than the letter, and goes far beyond its limits. One who clings to the letter or to a locution or to the form or figure of a vision,

which can be grasped, will not fail to go far astray and will immediately fall into great confusion and error, because he has guided himself by the senses according to these visions and not allowed the spirit to work in detachment from the senses. As Paul says: The letter kills and the spirit gives life. Therefore in this matter of the senses the letter must be set aside and the soul must remain in darkness, in faith, which is the spirit.

8.   So, in interpreting prophecy, we must not consider our own senses and language, knowing that God's language is different from ours and that it is spiritual language, far removed from our understanding.

9.   Who would fail to fall into confusion and to go astray if he confined himself to a literal interpretation of the prophecy that David spoke concerning Christ, in the seventy-first Psalm: He will have dominion from one sea even to the other sea, and from the river even unto the ends of the earth? In the same place he says: He will deliver the poor man from the power of the mighty, and the poor man who had no helper. But later Christ was born in a low estate and lived in poverty and died in misery. Not only did he have no dominion over the earth in a temporal sense while he lived, but also he was subject to lowly persons until he died under the power of Pontius Pilate. Not only did he not deliver poor men—that is, his disciples—from the hands of the mighty, in a temporal sense, but also he allowed them to be slain and persecuted for his name's sake.

10.   The fact is that these prophecies concerning Christ had to be understood spiritually, in which sense they were entirely

true. Christ was not only Lord of earth, but also of heaven, since he was God. And the poor who were to follow him he was not only to redeem and free from the power of the devil, that mighty one against whom they had no helper, but also to make heirs of the kingdom of heaven.

11. So God was speaking, in the most important sense, of Christ and of his followers' reward, which was an eternal kingdom and eternal freedom. They understood this in their own way as temporal dominion and temporal freedom, which in God's eyes is neither kingdom nor freedom at all. Therefore, being blinded by the insufficiency of the prophecy's literal meaning, and not understanding its spirit and truth, men took the life of their God and Lord. As Paul said: Those who dwelt in Jerusalem, and her rulers, not knowing who he was nor understanding the sayings of the prophets that are read every Sabbath day, have fulfilled them by judging him.

12. Although sayings and revelations may be of God we cannot always be sure of their meaning, for we can easily be greatly deceived by them because of our manner of understanding them. To try to limit them to what we can understand concerning them and to what our senses can grasp is like attempting to grasp the air and some particle in it that the hand touches: The air disappears and nothing remains.

13. The spiritual teacher must therefore do his best to see that the spirituality of his disciple is not cramped by attempts to interpret all supernatural things, which are no more than spiritual particles, for fear that he may retain nothing but these and have no spirituality at all. But let the teacher wean

his disciple from all visions and locutions and impress on him the necessity of dwelling in the freedom and darkness of faith, in which come spiritual freedom and abundance— and consequently the wisdom and understanding necessary to interpret God's words.

CHAPTER 15
Why it is not lawful under the law of grace to ask anything of God by supernatural means.

1. In Isaiah God rebukes the children of Israel because they desired to go down to Egypt without first inquiring of him, using these words: You did not ask first at my own mouth what was right. And we read in Joshua that when the children of Israel were deceived by the Gibeonites, the Holy Spirit rebuked them for this fault, saying: They ate of their food and they did not inquire at the mouth of God. Furthermore, we see in the Holy Scriptures that Moses always inquired of God, as did King David and all the kings of Israel with regard to their wars and needs, and the priests and prophets of old; and God answered and spoke with them and was not angry, and it was well done. If they did not do this it would be done poorly. Why, then, in the new law—the law of grace—may it not be now as it was before?

2. To this we must reply that the principal reason that in the law of Holy Scripture the inquiries made of God were lawful,

and why it was right for prophets and priests to seek visions and revelations of God, was that at that time faith had no firm foundation, neither was the law of the gospel established. So there was a need to inquire of God and for him to speak, whether by words or by visions and revelations or by many other ways of expressing his meaning. All that he spoke and revealed pertained to the mysteries of our faith and things touching it. Since the things of faith are not of mankind but come from the mouth of God himself, God himself rebuked them because they did not inquire at his mouth in his dealings, so that he might answer and might direct their affairs toward the faith.

3. At that time they had no knowledge of the faith, because it was not yet founded. But now that the faith is founded in Christ, and in this era of grace the law of the gospel has been made manifest, there is no reason to inquire of him in that manner, nor for him to answer as he did then. In giving us his Son, who is his Word—and he has no other— he spoke to us all together, once and for all, in this single Word, and he has no occasion to speak further.

4. This is the sense of that passage with which Paul begins when he tries to persuade the Hebrews that they should abandon their first ways of communication with God that are in the law of Moses, and should set their eyes on Christ alone. He said: That which God spoke of old in the prophets to our ancestors in various ways, he has now, at last, in these days, spoken to us once and for all in the Son. In this the apostle declares that God has become, so to speak, mute and has no more to say, since that which he spoke in

earlier times, in part to the prophets, he has now spoken altogether in Christ, giving us the All, which is his Son.

5. Therefore one who would now inquire of God or seek any vision or revelation would not only be acting foolishly, but would be committing an offense against God by not setting his eyes altogether on Christ and seeking nothing else.

6. God might answer him this way: If I have spoken everything to you in my Word, which is my Son, and I have no other word, what answer can I make to you now, or what can I reveal to you that is greater than this? For since the day that I descended upon him with my Spirit on the Mount of Transfiguration, saying: This is my beloved Son, in whom I am well pleased; listen to him, I have left off all these manners of teaching and answering, and I have entrusted this to him. Listen to him; for I have no more faith to reveal, neither do I have any more things to declare. If you want me to answer you with any word of consolation, consider my Son, who is subject to me and is bound by love for me and is afflicted, and you will see how fully he answers you. If you want me to explain secret things to you, set your eyes on him alone, and you will find the most secret mysteries and the wisdom and wondrous things of God, which are hidden in him.

7. Therefore anything received by the soul through supernatural means must clearly and plainly, fully and simply, be at once communicated to one's spiritual director. Although we have insisted so much that such things should be set aside and that confessors should not encourage their penitents to discuss them, it is not good for spiritual guides to show

displeasure in regard to them or to make their penitents afraid to mention them.

8.   Rather, there is a reason for proceeding quietly and kindly, encouraging these souls and giving them an opportunity to speak. If necessary, they must be exhorted to speak; in view of the difficulty that some souls experience in describing such matters, this is sometimes quite essential. Let confessors direct their penitents into faith and advise them to turn away their eyes from all such things, and give them to understand how much more precious in God's sight is one work or act of the will performed in charity than are all the visions and communications that they may receive from heaven, since these imply neither merit nor demerit. Let them point out, too, that many souls who have known nothing of such things have made incomparably greater progress than others who have received many of them.

CHAPTER 16

Things of the understanding may come in a purely spiritual way.

1.   We will now turn to the other four things of the understanding—that is, visions, revelations, locutions, and spiritual feelings. These we call purely spiritual, for they do not communicate themselves to the understanding by way of the physical senses. But without the intervention of any inward or outward physical sense, they present themselves

to the understanding, clearly and distinctly, by supernatural means, passively—that is to say, without the performance of any active act or operation on the part of the soul itself.

2. All four of these things may be called "visions of the soul," for we call the understanding of the soul its "sight." Since all these things are intelligible to the understanding, they are described in a spiritual sense as visible. The kinds of intelligence that are formed in the understanding may be called intellectual visions. All the objects of the other senses—sight, hearing, smell, taste, and touch—are objects of the understanding insofar as they fall within the limits of truth or falsehood. Just as to the eyes of the body all that is visible in a physical way causes physical vision, even so, to the spiritual eyes of the soul—that is, the understanding—all that is intelligible causes spiritual vision. For the soul to understand is for it to see.

3. We describe what the understanding receives by means of sight (because it can see things spiritually, even as the eyes can see physically) as a vision. What it receives by perceiving and understanding new things (so to speak through the hearing, when it hears things that are not heard) we describe as revelation. What it receives by means of hearing we call locution. What it receives through the other senses, such as the perception of sweet spiritual fragrance and spiritual taste and spiritual delight that the soul may enjoy supernaturally, we call spiritual feelings. From all these the soul derives spiritual vision or intelligence without any kind of perception concerning form, image, or figure of natural imagination. These things are communicated to the soul directly by a supernatural process.

CHAPTER 17
Two kinds of spiritual vision that come supernaturally.

1. Two kinds of vision can be received by the understanding: One kind is of physical substances; the other, of nonphysical substances. The physical visions have respect to all material things in heaven and on earth that the soul is able to see, even while still in the body, by the aid of a certain supernatural illumination derived from God, through which it is able to see all things that are not present, both in heaven and on earth. This was John's experience, as we read in the twenty-first chapter of Revelation where he relates the excellence that he saw of the heavenly Jerusalem.

2. The other visions, those of physical substances, cannot be seen by the aid of this derived illumination, but only by another, higher illumination: the illumination of glory. Such visions occur in this life only occasionally and fleetingly when God so allows it. At such times he totally withdraws the spirit from this life, and the natural functions of the body are supplied by his favor. This is why Paul was raptured at the time when he saw physical substances in the third heaven, and of what he saw he says that he does not know if it was in the body or out of the body, but that God knows. In this we clearly see that the limits of natural means of communication were bypassed, and that this was the work of God.

3. Let us now turn to the visions of physical substances received spiritually in the soul, which come in the same way as physical visions. Just as the eyes see physical visions by means of natural light, through the understanding the soul by means of supernaturally derived light sees those same natural things inwardly, as God wills. The difference between the two kinds of vision is only in the mode and manner of them. Now, spiritual and intellectual visions are much clearer and subtler than physical ones. When God is pleased to grant this favor to the soul, he communicates to it the supernatural light of which we speak, in which the soul sees easily and clearly the things that God wills it to see, whether of heaven or of earth. The absence or presence of them is no hindrance to the vision.

4. At times it is as though a door were opened before the soul into a great brightness, through which the soul sees a light like a lightning flash that on a dark night reveals things suddenly and causes them to be clearly and distinctly seen and then leaves them in darkness, although their forms and figures remain in the imagination. This happens much more perfectly in the soul, because the things the spirit has seen in that light remain impressed on it in such a way that whenever it observes them it sees them in itself as it saw them before.

5. The effect that these visions produce in the soul is that of quiet, illumination, joy like that of glory, sweetness, purity, love, humility, and elevation of the spirit in God.

6. The devil can also produce these visions by means of a certain natural light by which he brings things clearly

before the mind through spiritual suggestion, whether they are present or absent. But the effects produced in the soul by the devil's visions are not like those produced by good visions. The former produce dryness of spirit as to communion with God and an inclination to esteem oneself highly and to receive and set store by these visions. In no way do they produce the gentleness of humility and love of God. Neither do the forms of such visions remain impressed on the soul with the sweetness and brightness of the others. Nor do they last, but are quickly erased from the soul except when the soul greatly esteems them. In that case this high esteem itself causes it to recall them naturally, but with great dryness of spirit, and without producing the effect of love and humility that is produced by good visions when the soul recalls them.

7. These visions, inasmuch as they are of created things with which God has no essential conformity or proportion, cannot serve the understanding as a direct means to union with God. The soul must conduct itself in a purely negative way concerning them in order to progress by the direct means—that is, by faith. The more the soul desires obscurity and being reduced to nothing with respect to all the outward or inward things that it is capable of receiving, the more is it infused by faith, and consequently, by hope and love, since all these three theological virtues go together.

CHAPTER 18

The distinction between the two kinds of revelation.

1. The next thing to discuss is the second kind of spiritual perception, which we have described as revelation and which properly pertains to the spirit of prophecy. Revelation is nothing else than the discovery of some hidden truth or the manifestation of some secret or mystery. God may cause the soul to understand something by making clear to the understanding the truth concerning it, or he may reveal to the soul certain things that he proposes to do.

2. Accordingly, we may say that there are two kinds of revelation: The first is the disclosure to the understanding of truths that are properly called intellectual knowledge or intelligence. The second is the manifestation of secrets, which are called revelations more properly than the others. The first kind cannot strictly be called revelations, since they consist in this, that God causes the soul to understand plain truths, not only with respect to temporal things, but also with respect to spiritual things, revealing them to the soul clearly and openly.

3. This kind of vision (or, more properly, of knowledge of plain truths) is not like seeing physical things with the understanding. It consists rather in comprehending and seeing with the understanding the truths of God, whether of things that are, that have been, or that will be, which is in close conformity with the spirit of prophecy.

4. David, speaking for himself when something of this kind had happened to him, used only common and general terms, saying: God's judgments—that is, the virtues and attributes that we perceive in God—are in themselves true, justified, and more to be desired than gold, very much more than precious stones, and sweeter than the honeycomb and honey.

5. Concerning Moses we read that when God gave him a most lofty manifestation of Himself while passing before him, he said only what can be expressed in the common terms mentioned above. When the Lord passed before him in that manifestation of knowledge, Moses quickly prostrated himself on the ground, saying: Ruler, Lord, God, merciful and clement, patient, and of great compassion, and true, who keeps mercy promised unto thousands. Moses could not express what he had learned from God in one single manifestation of knowledge, and therefore he expressed it in all these words.

6. The second kind of vision of interior truths is of such a kind that when the soul learns these truths, they sink into it, independently of any suggestion from outside it. Yet, although the soul holds something that it understands to be quite certain, and although it may be unable to cease giving it passive interior consent, it must not as a result cease to believe and to give the consent of reason to what its spiritual director tells it, even though this may be contrary to its own feelings. In this way it may be directed in faith to divine union, to which a soul must journey by believing rather than by understanding.

Mysticism

7. In the Second Book of Kings we have an example that shows that spiritual persons may have knowledge of happenings even though they may occur elsewhere. Gehazi, Elisha's servant, wanted to hide from Elisha the money that he had received from Naaman the Syrian. But Elisha said: Was not my heart present when Naaman turned back from his chariot and went to meet you? This happens spiritually; the spirit sees it as though it were happening in its presence.

8. With regard to the deceptions that the devil brings about concerning this kind of knowledge and understanding there is much to say, for the deceptions that he effects in this way are many and are difficult to unmask. Through suggestion he can present to the soul many kinds of intellectual knowledge and implant them so firmly that it appears impossible for them not to be true.

9. At times the devil shows the soul others' sins, evil consciences, and evil souls, falsely but vividly, and he does all this to harm the soul, trusting that it will spread abroad his revelations and that more sins will be committed. Though it is true that God sometimes sets before holy souls the needs of their neighbors so that they may commend them to God or relieve them, even as we read that he revealed to Jeremiah the weakness of the prophet Baruch so that he might give him counsel concerning it, yet it is more often the devil who does this. The devil speaks falsely in order to cause infamy, sin, and discouragement.

10. The soul must always be scrupulous in rejecting these things and seek to journey to God by the way of unknowing. It must always relate its experiences to its spiritual confessor

and be always attentive to his counsel. Let the confessor guide the soul past this, laying no stress on it, for it is of no importance for the road to union. When these things are granted to the soul passively they always leave in it such effect as God wills to remain, without the need for the soul to exert any diligence in the matter.

CHAPTER 19

The second kind of revelation is the manifestation of hidden secrets.

1. The second kind of revelation is the manifestation of hidden mysteries and secrets. This may happen in two ways. The first is with respect to what God is in himself, including the revelation of the mystery of the Most Holy Trinity and Unity of God. The second is with respect to what God is in his works, and in this are included the other articles of our Catholic faith and propositions deducible from them that may be laid down explicitly as truths.

2. Under this second heading we may also include other things that God reveals concerning the world, in general as well as in particular, concerning kingdoms, provinces, states, families, and individuals.

3. As to these revelations that are included under our second heading, God still grants them in our time to whom he wills. For example, he may desire to reveal to some persons how many days they still have to live, or what trials they are to suffer, or what is to happen to such and such a person

or such and such a nation. Even as regards the mysteries of our faith, he will reveal to the spirit the truths concerning them, although since they have already been revealed, they are not properly termed revelations but more correctly manifestations or explanations of what has been revealed already.

4. In this kind of revelation the devil may meddle freely. Since revelations of this nature ordinarily come through words and figures, the devil may readily counterfeit others like them, much more so than when the revelations are in the spirit alone. Therefore, if, as touching our faith, anything new or different is revealed to us with regard to the first and second kinds of revelation that we are describing here, we must in no way give our consent to it even if we have evidence that an angel from heaven spoke it. As Paul says: Even though an angel from heaven were to declare or preach unto you anything else than what we have preached unto you, let him be anathema.

5. Since there are no more articles to be revealed concerning the substance of our faith than those that have already been revealed to the Church, not only must the soul reject anything new that may be revealed, but it behooves the soul to be cautious and pay no attention to any novelties implied in it, and for the sake of the soul's purity to rely on faith alone.

6. Therefore, the soul that is pure, cautious, simple, and humble must resist revelations and other visions with as much effort and care as though they were perilous temptations. There is no need to desire them. On the contrary, there is need

not to desire them if we are to reach the union of love. We have no need, in order to be perfect, to desire supernatural things by supernatural means that are above our capacity.

CHAPTER 20
Interior locutions may come to the spirit in one of three forms.

1. I will now turn to the third kind of perception, which is that of supernatural locutions that are apt to come to the minds of spiritual persons without the intervention of any physical sense. These may be reduced to three: successive, formal, and substantial.

2. I describe as successive certain words and arguments that the spirit desires to fashion when it is inwardly recollected.

3. Formal words are clear and distinct words that the spirit receives, not from itself, but from a third person, sometimes when it is recollected and sometimes when it is not.

4. Substantial words are others that also come to the mind formally, sometimes when it is recollected and sometimes when it is not; these cause in the soul the substance and virtue that they signify.

CHAPTER 21

The first kind of words that the recollected spirit sometimes forms within itself.

1. Successive words always come when the spirit is recollected and absorbed in some meditation. In its reflections on the subject at hand it proceeds from one stage to another, forming words and arguments that are much to the point, with great ease and distinctiveness. By means of its reasoning it discovers things that it did not know with respect to the subject of its reflections, so that it seems not to be doing this itself. Rather, it seems that another person is supplying the reasoning within its mind or answering its questions or teaching it. It has good cause for thinking this, for the soul is reasoning with itself and answering itself as though it were two persons convening together.

2. In some ways this is really so. Although it is the spirit itself that works as an instrument, the Holy Spirit often aids it to form its true reasoning, words, and conceptions. So it utters them to itself as though to a third person. At that time the understanding is recollected and united with the truth of the subject about which it is thinking, and the Holy Spirit is also united with it in that truth, as it is always united in all truth. Therefore it follows that when the understanding communicates in this way with the Holy Spirit by means of this truth, it begins to form within itself, successively, those other truths that are connected with the subject at hand. The door is opened to it and illumination is given to it continually by the Holy Spirit who teaches it.

3. Deception may, and does, frequently occur in the formal words and reasoning that the understanding bases on it. Inasmuch as the illumination that it receives is at times subtle and spiritual, so that the understanding cannot grasp it clearly, and it is the understanding that forms the reasoning of its own accord, it follows that those that it forms are frequently false, and on other occasions are only apparently true or are imperfect. Since at the outset the soul began to seize the truth, and then brought into play the skillfulness or the clumsiness of its own weak understanding, its perception of the truth may easily be modified by the instability of its own faculties of comprehension and act all the time exactly as though a third person were speaking.

4. I knew a person who had these successive locutions. Among them were some true and substantial ones concerning the most holy Sacrament of the Eucharist, but others were heresy. I am appalled at what happens in these days—that is, that some soul with the tiniest experience of meditation, if it is conscious of certain locutions of this kind in some state of recollection, at once christens them all as coming from God, assumes that this is the case, and says: God said to me . . . ; God answered me . . . ; whereas this is not the case at all, but for the most part it is they who are saying these things to themselves.

5. If you ask me why the understanding must be deprived of these truths, since through them it is illumined by the Spirit of God and thus they cannot be evil, I reply that the Holy Spirit illumines the recollected understanding according to the manner of its recollection, and that the understanding

cannot find any greater recollection than in faith. Therefore the Holy Spirit will illumine it in nothing more than in faith. The purer and the more refined in faith the soul is, the more it has of the infused charity of God. The more charity it has, the more it is illumined and the more gifts of the Holy Spirit are communicated to it, for charity is the means by which they are communicated to it.

6. If you tell me that this is all good, and that one does not impede the other, I reply that it impedes it greatly if the soul sets store by it. To do this is to occupy oneself with things that are of little importance, yet they are enough to hinder the communication of the chasm of faith in which God supernaturally and secretly instructs the soul and exalts it in virtues and gifts in a way that it is not aware of. The profit that these successive communications will bring us cannot come by our deliberately applying our understanding to them, for if we do this they will rather lead us astray, even as Wisdom says to the soul in the Song of Songs: Turn your away eyes from me, for they make me fly away.

7. Therefore we must not apply our understanding to what is being supernaturally communicated to us, but simply and sincerely apply our will to God with love. For it is through love that these good things are communicated, and through love they will be communicated in greater abundance than before.

8. There are certain minds that are so quick and subtle that when they become recollected during meditation, they invent conceptions and begin naturally and with great facility to form these conceptions into the most lifelike words and arguments, which—they think—without any doubt come

from God. Yet all the time they come only from the under-standing, which, with its natural illumination being to some extent freed from the operation of the senses, is able to effect all this and more without any supernatural aid.

9. Let these persons learn to be intent on nothing except only on grounding the will in humble love, working diligently, and through suffering imitating the Son of God in his life and mortifications. It is by this road that one will come to all spiritual good, rather than by much inward reasoning.

10. These successive locutions may proceed in the understand-ing from three causes: from the Holy Spirit, who moves and illumines the understanding; from the natural illumination of the understanding; and from the devil, who may speak to the soul by suggestion.

11. Let us remember this necessary caution, both as to one type of locution and as to the other, so that we may not be deceived or hindered by them. Let us treasure none of them, but think only of learning to direct our will determinedly to God, fulfilling his law and his holy counsels perfectly, which is the wisdom of the saints, and contenting ourselves with knowing the mysteries and truths that the Church sets truthfully and simply before us.

CHAPTER 22
The harm that may be done by interior words.

1. The interior words pertaining to the second type are formal words, which at certain times come to the spirit

by supernatural means without the intervention of any of the senses, sometimes when the spirit is recollected and at other times when it is not. I call them formal because they are communicated to the spirit formally by a third person, the spirit itself playing no part in this. They are therefore quite different from those that we have just described. Not only is there this difference—that they come without any such intervention of the spirit itself as takes place in the other case—but also they sometimes come when the spirit is not recollected and even when it is far from thinking about what is being said to it.

2. These words are sometimes clearly formed and sometimes less so. Frequently they are like conceptions in which something is said to the spirit, whether in the form of a reply to it or in that of another manner of address. Sometimes there is only one word; sometimes there are two or more. Sometimes the words succeed one another like those already described, for they are apt to be continuous, either instructing the soul or discussing something with it. All this happens without any part being played in it by the spirit, for it is just as though one person were speaking with another. This is what happened to Daniel, who says that an angel spoke within him. This was a formal and successive discourse within his spirit, which instructed him, just as the angel declared at the time by saying that he had come to instruct him.

3. When these words are no more than formal, the effect that they produce on the soul is not great. Ordinarily they serve only to instruct or illumine with respect to one thing. In

order to produce this effect, it is not necessary for them to produce any greater effect than the purpose to which they are leading. When they are of God they invariably work this in the soul: They make it ready and quick to do what it is instructed to do.

4. On the other hand, when the words and communications are of the devil, the soul responds more readily to greater things and dislikes lowlier things. God so abhors seeing souls attracted by high position that even when he obliges them to accept such positions he does not want them to be anxious to command.

5. The readiness that God commonly inspires in the soul through formal words constitutes one great difference between them and successive words. The latter do not move the spirit as much, neither do they inspire it with as much readiness, since they are less formal and the understanding has more to do with them. Nevertheless successive words may sometimes produce a greater effect because of the close communication that there is at times between the Holy Spirit and the human spirit.

6. It is in the manner of their coming that there is a great difference between the two kinds of locution. With respect to formal words the soul can have no doubt as to whether it is pronouncing them itself, for it sees readily that it is not, especially when it has not been thinking about what has been said. Even when it has been thinking along those lines it feels clearly and distinctly that the words come from elsewhere.

7. The soul must attach no more importance to formal words than to successive words. Apart from the fact that to do so

would occupy the spirit with what is not a legitimate and direct means to union with God, that is, faith, it might also easily cause it to be deceived by the devil.

8.   The soul, then, must take no account of what these words may express, or attach any importance to them, no matter whether the spirit from which they come is good or evil. The words must be repeated to an experienced confessor or to a discreet and learned person, so that person may give instruction and impart advice. If such an expert person cannot be found, it is better to attach no importance to these words and to repeat them to no one, for it is easy to find persons who will ruin the soul rather than edify it. Souls must not be given into the charge of just any kind of director, since in so grave a matter it is of the greatest importance whether one goes astray or acts rightly.

9.   A soul should never act according to its own opinion or accept anything of what these locutions express without much reflection and without taking the advice of another person. Strange and subtle deceptions may arise in this matter, so much so that I believe that the soul that does not set itself against accepting such things cannot fail to be deceived by many of them.

CHAPTER 23
The difference between substantial words and formal words.

1. The third kind of interior words is called substantial. Substantial words, which are also formal in that they are impressed on the soul in a definitely formal way, are nevertheless different, for substantial words produce vivid and substantial effects on the soul, whereas merely formal words do not. Although it is true that every substantial word is formal, every formal word is not therefore substantial, but only such a word as impresses substantially on the soul what it signifies.

2. It is as if Our Lord were to say formally to the soul: Be good. Then it would be substantially good. Or as if he were to say: Love me. Then it would have within itself the substance of love for God. Or as if it were greatly afraid and he said: Do not be afraid. At once it would feel within itself great fortitude and tranquility. God's word is full of power. So what he says to the soul he produces substantially within it.

3. This was so with Abraham, when God said to him: Walk in my presence and be faultless. He was then faultless and walked ever in the fear of God. This is the power of God's word in the Gospels, which show that he healed the sick and raised the dead by no more than a word. In the same way he gives certain souls substantial locutions that are of such import and price that they are life, virtue, and

incomparable good to the soul. One of these words works greater good within the soul than all that the soul itself has done throughout its life.

4. With respect to these words, the soul should do nothing. It should neither desire them nor refrain from desiring them; it should neither reject them nor fear them. It should do nothing in the way of executing what these words express, for God never pronounces substantial words so that the soul may translate them into action, but so that he may translate them within the soul. This is how they differ from formal and successive words.

5. Let the soul rather be resigned and humble with respect to these words. It must not reject them, since their effect remains substantially within it and is full of the good that comes from God. As the soul receives this good passively, the soul's action is never of any importance. Nor should it fear any deception. Neither the understanding nor the devil can intervene in this, nor can they succeed in passively producing a substantial effect in the soul in such a way that the effect of the locution will be impressed on it. In many things and even on good souls the devil works great violence by means of suggestion, making his suggestions effective. If they were evil he might work in them the carrying out of these suggestion, but he cannot leave on a soul effects similar to those of good locutions.

6. There is no comparison between the locutions of the devil and those of God. In comparison with the latter, the former are all as though they did not exist, and they do not produce any effect at all compared with the effect of the

latter. As God says through Jeremiah: What has the chaff to do with the wheat? Are not my words perhaps as fire, and as a hammer that breaks the rock in pieces? So substantial words are greatly conducive to the soul's union with God. The more interior they are, the more substantial they are, and the greater is the profit that they bring. Happy is the soul to whom God addresses these words. Speak, Lord, for your servant is listening.

CHAPTER 24
The things received by the understanding from interior feelings.

1. It is now time to turn to the fourth and last kind of intellectual perception. These might come to the understanding through the spiritual feelings that are often produced supernaturally in the souls of spiritual persons. We count them among the distinct aspects of the understanding.

2. These distinct spiritual feelings may be of two kinds. The first is in the affection of the will, and the second is in the substance of the soul. Each of these itself may be of many kinds. Those of the will, when they are from God, are most sublime. Those that are from the substance of the soul are high and of great good and profit. Neither the soul nor one who deals with it can know or understand the cause from which they proceed, or the acts by which God may grant it these favors. They depend neither on any works performed

by the soul nor on its meditations, although both these things are a good preparation for them: God grants these favors to whom he wills and for what reason he wills.

3. These feelings, inasmuch as they are only feelings, do not pertain to the understanding but to the will. From these feelings, both from those of the will and from those that are in the substance of the soul, whether they are caused suddenly by God's touches or are durable and successive, a perception of knowledge or intelligence frequently overflows into the understanding. This is normally a most sublime perception of God, most delectable to the understanding, to which no name can be given any more than to the feeling from which it overflows.

4. As is the case with successive locutions, the activity of the understanding would easily disturb and ruin the effect of these delicate manifestations of knowledge, which are a delectable supernatural intelligence that human nature cannot grasp through its own efforts, but only through remaining in a state of receptivity. The soul must not strive to receive them for fear that the understanding should form other manifestations of its own, or the devil should make his entry with still more that are different from them and false. This he may well do by means of the feelings mentioned above, or by those that he can himself infuse into the soul that devotes itself to these kinds of knowledge.

5. Let the soul be resigned, humble, and passive in this, for since it receives this knowledge passively from God, God will communicate it whenever he pleases to the soul that is

humble and detached. In this way the soul will do nothing to counteract the great help that these kinds of knowledge give it in its progress toward divine union. These touches are all touches of union, which is worked passively in the soul.

BOOK THREE

Book Three describes the purging of the active night of the memory and the will. It tells how the soul is to behave with respect to these two faculties so that it may come to union with God in perfect hope and charity.

The soul must purify the memory and the will.

1. The first faculty of the soul—the understanding—has now been instructed in faith, the first theological virtue, so that through this faculty the soul may be united with God by means of the purity of faith. Now we must do the same thing with respect to the other two faculties of the soul, which are memory and will, and purify them also. Through these two faculties as well, the soul may come to union with God in perfect hope and charity. If the spiritual person instructs the understanding in faith according to the doctrine that has been given, he will instruct the other two faculties in the other two virtues also. The operations of each faculty depend on the others.

2. Now we must set down the things proper to each faculty, starting with the memory. This we will do by looking at their three objects: natural, imaginary, and spiritual. We will start with the kinds of knowledge that come from the memory: natural and supernatural, imaginary and spiritual.

CHAPTER 2

The soul must be emptied of the natural things of the memory.

1. Natural knowledge in the memory consists in all the kinds of knowledge that the memory can form concerning the objects of the five physical senses—hearing, sight, smell, taste, and touch. The soul must empty itself of all these forms of knowledge and strive to lose their imaginary achievements, so that there may be left in it no impression of knowledge or the trace of anything at all. Rather, the soul must remain barren, as if these forms had never passed through it, and in total forgetfulness and suspension.

2. This cannot happen unless the memory is reduced to nothing in all its forms in order to be united with God. It cannot happen except by total separation from everything that is not God. God does not come under any definite form or kind of knowledge in dealing with the night of the understanding. Christ says: No one can serve two masters. So the memory cannot be united both with God and with knowledge. Since God has no form or image that can be

comprehended by the memory, then when the memory is united with God it remains without form. Divine union empties its imagination, sweeps it clean of all forms of knowledge, and raises it to the supernatural.

3. Because of the memory's union with God, sometimes forgetfulness of the memory and suspension of the imagination reach such a point that a long time passes without the soul's perceiving it or knowing what has taken place during that period. Since the faculty of imagination is then in suspension, it feels nothing that is done to it, not even things that cause pain. These suspensions do not happen in those who are already mature since they have attained to perfect union, while these suspensions pertain to the beginnings of union.

4. One may remark that all this looks good, but it leads to the destruction of the natural use of the faculties and reduces mankind to the state of a beast since one becomes incapable of reasoning or remembering his natural functions and needs. I will argue that God does not destroy nature, but rather perfects it.

5. The operations of the soul in divine union are from the Holy Spirit; the actions of such souls are only those that are seemly and reasonable. God's Spirit teaches them what they ought to know and causes them to be ignorant of what they ought not to know, to remember what they have to remember, and to forget what they should forget. It makes them love what they have to love, and not to love what does not pertain to God. The first motions of the faculties of such souls are divine, and we must not wonder at this since they are transformed in the Divine Being.

6. The spiritual person needs habitually to practice caution: Everything that he hears, sees, smells, tastes, or touches, he must be careful not to store up or collect in his memory, but he must allow himself to forget them immediately. This he must accomplish, if need be, with the same effectiveness as that which others use to remember them. As a result no knowledge or image of them remains in his memory.

CHAPTER 3

Three evils come to the soul when it uses natural knowledge and the memory.

1. The spiritual person is subject to three kinds of evil when he persists in desiring to make use of natural knowledge and the memory to journey toward God—or for any other purpose. Two of these are positive and one is privative. The first comes from things of the world; the second comes from the devil; the third, the privative, is the hindrance to divine union that the soul causes and puts into effect.

2. The first evil, which comes from the world, consists in the soul's subjection, through knowledge and reflection, to many kinds of harm, such as falsehoods, imperfections, desires, opinions, loss of time, and many other things that breed impurity in the soul. The soul must of necessity fall into perils of falsehood when it allows the entrance of knowledge and reasoning. Often what is true appears false, and what is certain, doubtful, and vice-versa, for there is

hardly one single truth of which we can have complete knowledge. The soul is free from all these things if the memory enters into darkness with respect to every kind of reflection and knowledge.

3. Imperfections meet the soul at every step if it sets the memory on what it has heard, seen, touched, smelled, and tasted. If it does, some sort of feeling has to cling to it, whether pain, fear, hatred, vain hope, or vain enjoyment. At the least these are imperfections, and at times they are downright sins. Subtly they leave much impurity in the soul, even though the reflections and the knowledge have relation to God.

4. These things engender desires within the soul, for they arise naturally from knowledge and reflections; if one merely wishes to have knowledge and reflections, even that is a desire. Many occasions of judging others will also come, since in using its memory, the soul cannot fail to discover the good and the bad in others. In such a case, what is evil often seems good, and what is good, evil. There is no one who can completely free himself from all these kinds of evil, except by blinding the memory and leading it into darkness with regard to all these things.

5. Let the soul, then, remain "enclosed," without anxieties and troubles; and the One who entered in physical form to his disciples when the doors were shut and gave them peace, though they neither thought that this was possible nor knew how it was possible, will enter spiritually into the soul without its knowing how he does so, when the doors of its faculties—memory, understanding, and will—

are enclosed against all things. He will fill them with peace coming down on the soul, as the prophet says, like a river, taking it from all the misgivings, suspicions, disturbances, and darkness that caused it to fear that it was lost or was on the way to being so. Let it not grow careless about prayer, and let it wait in detachment from the world and in emptiness, for its blessings will not be long in coming.

CHAPTER 4
The second evil that may come to the soul from the natural things of the memory.

1. The second positive evil that may come to the soul by means of the knowledge of the memory proceeds from the devil, who uses it to obtain great influence over the soul. He can continually bring to it new forms, knowledge, and reflections, by means of which he can taint the soul with pride, avarice, wrath, and envy, and cause it unjust hatred or vain love, and deceive it in many ways. Besides this, he desires to leave impressions in the imagination in such a way that those that are false appear true, and those that are true, false. In the end, all the worst deceptions the devil causes and the evils that he brings to the soul enter by way of the memory. If the memory enters into darkness with respect to them all and is reduced to nothing in its forgetfulness to them, it shuts the door altogether on this evil from the devil and frees itself from all these things. This is a great blessing.

2. I want spiritual persons to see clearly how many kinds of harm are worked by evil spirits in their souls by means of the memory when they devote themselves frequently to making use of it, and how many kinds of sadness and affliction and vain and evil joys they have, both with respect to their thoughts about God and with respect to the things of the world. I want them to see how many impurities are left rooted in their spirits, and how greatly they are distracted from the highest recollection, which consists in fixing the entire soul, according to its faculties, on the one incomprehensible Good, and in withdrawing it from all things that can be perceived.

CHAPTER 5

The third evil that may come to the soul through distinct natural knowledge or the memory.

1. The third evil that comes to the soul through the natural memory is privative, for its perceptions can hinder moral good and deprive us of spiritual good. How do these things hinder moral good in the soul? Moral good consists in restraining the passions and curbing disorderly desires. From this restraint, tranquility, peace, rest, and moral virtues come to the soul—all of which things are moral good. The soul that does not forget things pertaining to itself and does not withdraw itself from them cannot truly restrain the passions. No disturbances ever arise in the soul

except through the memory. When all things are forgotten, there is nothing that can disturb peace or that moves the desires. What the eye does not see the heart does not desire.

2. This we are constantly learning by experience. Whenever the soul begins to think about any subject it is moved and disturbed, either much or little, with respect to that subject, according to its nature. If it is a troublesome and grievous matter, the soul finds sadness in it; if it is pleasant, the soul finds desire and joy. The result is necessarily disturbance: The soul is now joyful, now sad; now it hates, now it loves. It cannot continue in one and the same attitude (which is an effect of moral tranquility) except when it strives to forget all things.

CHAPTER 6

The benefits that come to the soul from emptiness of thoughts and knowledge.

1. First, the soul enjoys tranquility and peace of mind since it is freed from the disturbance and changeableness that arise from the memory. Consequently—and this is more important—it enjoys purity of conscience and soul.

2. Second, the soul is freed from suggestions, temptations, and motions of the devil, who insinuates these things into the soul by means of thoughts, causing it to fall into impurities and sins. When these thoughts have been completely removed, the devil has nothing he can use to assault the soul by natural means.

3. Third, through recollecting itself and forgetting all things the soul is inwardly prepared for the Holy Spirit to move and teach it.

4. Solomon, being well acquainted with both the evil and the benefit of the things we are speaking about, said: I knew that there was nothing better for mankind than to rejoice and to do good in life. By this he meant that in everything that happens to us, however adverse it may be, we should rejoice rather than be disturbed, so that we may not lose a blessing that is greater than any kind of prosperity—that is, tranquility and peace of mind in all things.

CHAPTER 7
One kind of perception of the memory.

The soul must never reflect on the distinct objects that may have passed through its mind by supernatural means, in such a way as to preserve within itself the forms and figures and knowledge of those things. We must always bear in mind this principle: The more attention the soul pays to any object whether natural or supernatural, the less capacity and preparation it has for entering into the chasm of faith, in which everything else is absorbed.

CHAPTER 8

Many evils may come to the soul by reflecting on supernatural things.

1. The spiritual person incurs the risk of five kinds of evil if he devotes attention to the ideas impressed on him by the things that pass through his mind in a supernatural way.

2. First, he is frequently deceived and mistakes one thing for another. Second, he is in danger of falling into some form of presumption or vanity. Third, the devil has many occasions of deceiving him using the things mentioned above. Fourth, he is hindered as to union in hope with God. Fifth, for the most part he has a low judgment of God.

3. As to the first evil, if the spiritual person devotes attention to these notions and reflects on them, he must frequently be deceived in his judgment of them. One can have neither a complete understanding of the things that pass naturally through the imagination nor a perfect and certain judgment about them. One will be less able still to have these with respect to supernatural things, which are above our capacity to understand and occur only rarely. Therefore such a person will often think that what actually comes only from his imagination is from God. Yet often what seems to be from God is from the devil, and what seems to be from the devil is from God.

4. Therefore the spiritual person should not desire to apply judgment in order to know the nature of his own condition or feelings, or the nature of any vision, idea, or feeling.

He should not even desire to know it or to pay attention to it. This he should desire only in order to speak of it to his spiritual director and to be taught how to empty his memory of these things.

CHAPTER 9

The peril of falling into self-esteem and vain presumption.

1. Supernatural objects of the memory are also a frequent occasion for spiritual persons to fall into presumption or vanity, if they devote attention to them and set store by them. Just as one who knows nothing of them is free from falling into this vice, seeing that he has no opportunity for presumption, one who has experience with them has close at hand an occasion for thinking himself to be somebody important since he possesses these supernatural communications. Although it is true that he may attribute them to God, hold himself to be unworthy of them, and give God the thanks, nevertheless a certain secret satisfaction remains in his spirit along with self-esteem and a sense of their value, from which, without him knowing it, great spiritual pride will come to him.

2. Consider the aversion such persons feel toward anyone who does not praise their spirituality, or esteem the experiences they enjoy and the mortification they suffer, when they find that others have just those same experiences or

even superior ones. All this arises from secret self-esteem and pride, and they can never quite realize that they are steeped in pride up to their eyes.

3. Such persons are like the Pharisee who gave thanks to God that he was not like other men and that he practiced many virtues, and was satisfied with himself and presumptuous. Although such persons may not use the Pharisee's actual words, they resemble him in spirit. After the manner of the Pharisee they consider those who are not like themselves to be lowly and despicable.

4. To flee from this pernicious evil, so abhorrent in God's eyes, they must consider two things. First, virtue does not consist in perceptions and feelings concerning God, however sublime they may be, or in anything of this kind. On the contrary, virtue has nothing to do with feeling: It consists in a firmly rooted and keenly felt humility and contempt of oneself and of all that pertains to oneself. It also consists in not wishing to be of any account in the esteem of others.

5. Second, all visions, revelations, and feelings coming from heaven and any thoughts that may proceed from them are worth less than the smallest act of humility. Humility is one of the effects of charity, which thinks evil only of itself; it does not think anything good of itself, but only of others. Therefore it is good for supernatural things not to attract one's eyes; one should strive to forget them in order to be free.

CHAPTER 10
An evil that may come to the soul through imaginary perceptions.

1. Great evil may come to the soul from the devil by way of these supernatural things. He can present to the memory and the imagination false ideas that seem true and good, impressing them on the spirit and the senses with great effectiveness, and certifying them to be true by means of suggestion (so that it appears to the soul that it cannot be otherwise, but that everything is just as he presents it; for as he transfigures himself into an angel of light, he appears as light to the soul).

2. The devil may also tempt the soul in many ways with respect to true knowledge that is of God, moving its desires and affections, whether spiritual or sensual, in an unruly fashion with respect to supernatural things. If the soul takes pleasure in such things, it is easy for the devil to cause its desires and affections to grow within it and to make it fall into spiritual gluttony and other evils.

3. The better to do this, he suggests and gives pleasure, sweetness, and delight to the senses with respect to these same things of God, so that the soul is corrupted and disoriented by that sweetness, is blinded with that pleasure, sets its eyes on pleasure rather than on love (or at least much more than on love), and pays more attention to these aspects than to the detachment from the world and the emptiness that are found in faith, hope, and love of God. From this the devil

may go on gradually to deceive the soul and cause it easily to believe his falsehoods.

4. To the blind soul falsehood no longer appears to be falsehood and evil does not appear to be evil. Darkness appears to be light, and light, darkness. As a result that soul comes to commit a thousand foolish errors, whether with respect to natural things, or moral things, or spiritual things. Thus what was once sweet wine to it becomes sour vinegar. All this happens to the soul because it did not begin from the start by denying itself the pleasure of those supernatural things. At first this is a small matter and not harmful, so the soul has no misgivings and allows it to continue. But like the grain of mustard seed it grows into a tall tree. A small error at the beginning becomes a great error in the end.

5. Therefore, in order to flee from the great evil that comes from the devil, the soul must not desire to have any pleasure in such things, because such pleasure will most surely lead it to become blind and to fall. Of their own nature and without the devil's help, pleasure and delight and sweetness blind the soul. This was David's meaning when he said: Perhaps darkness will blind me in my delights and I will have the night for my light.

CHAPTER 11

The hindrance that the soul places between itself and union.

1. For the soul to come to union with God in hope it must renounce every possession of the memory. For its hope in God to be perfect, it must have nothing in the memory that is not God. Whether of heaven or of earth, or whether natural or supernatural, no form or figure or image or other kind of knowledge that may come to the memory can take God's place or be like him. As David teaches: Lord, among the gods there is none like you.

2. Therefore, if the memory desires to notice any of these things, it hinders the soul from reaching God: first because it encumbers it, and next because the more the soul has of possession the less it has of hope. Therefore the soul must be stripped of the distinct forms and knowledge of supernatural things and become oblivious to them, so that the memory may not hinder its union with God in perfect hope.

CHAPTER 12

Another evil: a low and unseemly judgment of God.

1. No less serious is the fifth evil that comes to the soul from its desire to retain in the memory the images of things that are supernaturally communicated to it, above all if it desires

to use them as a means to divine union. It is easy to judge the Being and greatness of God less worthily and nobly than befits his incomprehensible nature. Our judgment may form no express conception that God is like any one of these things, yet esteeming these things causes it not to esteem God or not to feel concerning him as highly as faith teaches; for faith tells us that he is incomparable and incomprehensible.

2. Created things whether earthly or heavenly, and all images and kinds of knowledge whether natural or supernatural, that can be encompassed by the faculties of the soul, however lofty they may be in this life, have no comparison to God's Being. For God falls within no genus or species, whereas created things do. The soul in this life is not capable of receiving distinctly anything except what falls within genus and species. That is why John says that no person has seen God at any time, Isaiah says it has not entered into the heart of mankind what God is like, and God told Moses that he could not see God while he was in this mortal state. One who encumbers his memory and the other faculties of the soul with what they can comprehend cannot esteem God as he ought.

3. Let us make a comparison on a lower level. The more a person fixes his eyes on the king's servants and takes notice of them, the less notice he takes of the king himself and the less he esteems him. Although this comparison may not be distinctly present in the understanding it is inherent in the act, since the more attention the person gives to the servants the more he takes away from their lord. He cannot

have a high opinion of the king if the servants appear to him to be of any importance while they are in the presence of their lord. This is how the soul treats God when it devotes attention to created things. That is why they must all be banished from sight and the soul must withdraw its gaze from them so it may gaze on God through faith and hope.

⌐ CHAPTER 13 ⌐

The benefits of banishing the perceptions of the imagination.

1. Some benefits come from emptying the imagination of the forms that these five evils inflict on the soul if it desires to retain them. Apart from these there are other benefits for the spirit—that is, great rest and quiet. Setting aside the natural rest that the soul obtains when it is free from images and forms, the soul also becomes free from anxiety about whether they are good or evil and about how it must behave with respect to them both. Nor must it waste its spiritual guides' time by requiring them to decide if these things are good or evil and if they are of this kind or of another.

2. The soul has no need to desire to know all this if it devotes no attention to imaginary forms. It can better use the time and energies that it would have wasted in dealing with these images in another more profitable practice, that of the will with respect to God, and in taking care to seek both detachment from the world and poverty of spirit and sense.

The more the soul withdraws itself completely from all figures of the imagination, the more it will approach God.

3. One may ask: "Why do many spiritual persons counsel the soul to strive to profit by communications that come from God and to desire to receive them from him so that it may have something to give him? If he gives us nothing, will we give him nothing also? Why does Paul say: Do not quench the spirit? And the Bridegroom to the Bride: Set me as a seal on your heart and as a seal on your arm? Certainly this denotes some kind of perception. Surely since God gives it, he gives it for a good reason and it will have a good effect. We must not throw away pearls. It is even a kind of pride to be unwilling to receive the things of God, as if we could do without them and were self-sufficient."

4. To meet this objection we must recall that the good that overflows in the soul from supernatural perceptions, when they come from a good source, is produced passively in the soul at the instant they are presented to the senses, without the working of any operation of the faculties. Therefore it is unnecessary for the will to perform the act of receiving them.

5. The substance and the spirit unite with the faculties of the soul in true understanding and love only when at last the operation of the faculties ceases. Therefore, the difference between active and passive operation, and the superiority of the latter, correspond to the difference between what is being done and what is done already, or between what a person tries to effect and what is already effected.

6. If the soul should desire to employ its faculties actively on these supernatural things, the spirit of which God bestows

passively, it would be doing nothing less than abandoning what it had already done in order to do it again. It would not enjoy what it had done or produce any other result by these actions of its own except that of impeding what has been done already. The soul would be directly quenching the spirituality that God infuses through the imaginary perceptions mentioned above, if it were to set any store by them. Therefore it must set them aside and take up a passive and negative attitude with regard to them. At that time God is moving the soul to things above its own power and knowledge.

7. This is why the prophet said: I will stand on my watch and set my step on my tower, and I will watch to see what will be said to me. It is as if he were to say: I will stand on guard over my faculties and will take no step forward as to my actions, and so I will be able to contemplate what will be said to me—that is, I will understand and enjoy what is communicated to me supernaturally.

8. The passage that has been quoted concerning the Bridegroom is to be understood as referring to the love that he entreats of the Bride. The function of the love between two lovers is to make one like the other in the most vital part of them. Therefore he tells her to set him as a seal on her heart, which all the arrows strike that leave the quiver of love, arrows that are the actions and motives of love. They will all strike him who is there as a mark for them; so all will be for him, so that the soul will become like him through the actions and motions of love until it is transformed in him. He bids her set him as a seal on her arm because the arm performs the practice of love, sustaining and comforting the Beloved.

9. The figures that produce effects such as these are deeply implanted in the soul and are not like other images and forms retained in the imagination. So the soul has no need to have recourse to this faculty when it desires to recall them, for it sees that it has them within itself and that they are as an image seen in a mirror.

10. Only with great difficulty can it be known when these images are imprinted on the soul and when on the imagination. Those that touch the imagination are as apt to occur frequently as are the others; for certain persons are accustomed to having visions that take place in the mind and the imagination, visions presented to them in one form with great frequency. We may know them by their effects. Those that are natural or that come from the devil produce no good effect on the soul, however frequently it recalls them, nor work its spiritual renewal. Contemplating them simply produces dryness of soul. The good ones, however, produce some good effect when they are recalled.

11. One who has experienced these things will readily distinguish one kind from the other. I will add that those that are formally and durably imprinted on the soul are of rare occurrence. But whether they are of one kind or of another it is good for the soul to desire to understand nothing but God alone, through faith, in hope. To reject these things, if they are good, appears to be pride. But it is not so, for it is prudent humility to profit by them in the best way and to be guided by what is safest.

CHAPTER 14
The general method for governing oneself with respect to the memory.

1. It will be good at this point to give an account of the universal method that one must observe in order to be united with God according to memory. Our aim is the union of the soul with God in hope, according to the memory. Since what is hoped for is not possessed, and since the less we possess other things the greater scope and the greater capacity we have for hoping, and consequently the greater our hope, therefore, the more things we possess, the less scope and capacity we have for hoping, and consequently the less hope we have. The more the soul dispossesses the memory of forms and things that are not God, the more it will set its memory on God, and the emptier will its memory become, so that it may hope for the One who will fill it.

2. This doctrine of ours does not agree with the doctrine of bothersome persons, who, inspired by satanic pride and envy, desire to remove from the eyes of the faithful the holy and necessary use and the worthy adoration of images of God and the saints. We do not say here, as they do, that images should not exist and should not be adored; we simply explain the difference between images and God.

3. We exhort people to pass beyond the surface so that they may not be hindered from reaching the living truth behind it, and to make no more account of the superficial than is necessary for reaching the spiritual. Images are means

that serve to remind us of God and of the saints. When we attend to the means more than is necessary, they disturb and hinder us as much, in their own way, as anything else. This is all the more so when we turn to supernatural visions and images with respect to which many deceptions and perils arise.

4. With respect to the remembrance and esteem of images that the Church sets before us, there can be no deception or peril, because nothing is esteemed in them other than what is presented. Nor does remembering them fail to profit the soul, since they are not preserved in the memory except with love for what they represent. Provided the soul devotes no more attention to them than is necessary for this purpose, they will always assist it to union with God, allowing the soul to soar upward (when God grants it that favor) from the superficial image to the living God, forgetting every created thing and everything that pertains to created things.

CHAPTER 15
The dark night of the will.

1. We would have accomplished nothing by purging the understanding in order to ground it in the virtue of faith, and by purging the memory in order to ground it in hope, if we did not also purge the will according to the third virtue, which is charity. For it is by charity that the works that are done in faith have great merit, and without it they are of no worth. As James says: Without works of charity, faith is dead.

2. As we turn to the will's active detachment from the world and night in order to form it and make it perfect in this virtue of God's charity, I find no more fitting authority than what is written in the sixth chapter of Deuteronomy, where Moses says: You shall love the Lord your God with all your heart and with all your soul and with all your strength. These words contain all that the spiritual person ought to do and all that I have to teach him, so that he may truly reach God, by union of the will, through charity.

3. The soul's strength consists in its faculties, passions, and desires, all of which are governed by the will. When these are directed by the will toward God and turned away from all that is not God, the soul's strength is reserved for God. Then the soul is able to love God with all its strength.

4. So that the soul may do this, we will now turn to purging from the will all its unruly affections, from which arise unruly operations, affections, and desires, and from which also arises its failure to keep all its strength for God. These affections and passions are four: joy, hope, grief, and fear. When the passions are controlled by reason according to God's way, the soul rejoices only in God's honor and glory. It hopes for nothing else and fears nothing except God alone. The more the soul rejoices in anything other than God, the less completely it will center its rejoicing in God; the more it hopes in anything else, the less it will hope in God.

5. These four passions have the greater dominion in the soul and assail it the more vehemently when the will is less strongly attached to God and more dependent on created things. Then it rejoices readily at things that are not worthy

of joy, hopes in things that bring no profit, grieves over things in which it perhaps ought to rejoice, and fears where there is no reason for fearing.

6.   When these affections are unbridled, there arise in the soul all the vices and imperfections that it possesses, and when they are ordered and composed, all its virtues. If one of them should become ordered and controlled by reason, the rest will become so also. These four passions of the soul are so closely and intimately united to one another that the actual direction of one is the virtual direction of the others: If one is recollected the other three will virtually and proportionately be recollected also.

7.   If the will rejoices in anything, it will as a result hope for the same thing to the extent of its rejoicing; the same is true of grief and fear. To the extent that desire for that thing goes away, fear and grief concerning it also gradually go away, and hope for it goes away as well.

8.   The will with these four passions is portrayed by the figure that was seen by Ezekiel of four creatures with one body but four faces. The wings of one were joined to those of the others, and each one went straight before his face; when they went forward they did not turn back. In the same manner the wings of each one of these affections are joined to those of each of the others, so that in whichever direction one of them turns—that is, in its operation—the others must go also. When one of them descends they must all descend, and when one is lifted up they will all be lifted up. Where your hope is, there your joy and fear and grief will go. If your hope returns, the others will return.

9.   Therefore wherever one of these passions is directed, that is where the whole soul and the will and the other faculties will go, and they will all live as captives to this passion. The other three passions will be living in it also, afflicting the soul with their captivity and not allowing it to fly upward to the freedom and rest of sweet contemplation and union. As long as these passions reign, they do not allow the soul to remain in the tranquility and peace that are necessary for the wisdom that, by natural or supernatural means, it is capable of receiving.

CHAPTER 16
Joy may arise from six kinds of blessings.

1.   The first of the passions of the soul and affections of the will is joy, which is nothing other than satisfaction of the will, together with esteem for something that it considers desirable. The will never rejoices except when an object affords it appreciation and satisfaction. This is true of active joy, which arises when the soul clearly and distinctly understands the reason for its rejoicing, and when it is in its own power to rejoice or not. There is another, passive joy, a condition in which the will may find itself rejoicing without understanding clearly and distinctly the reason for its rejoicing, and occurring at times when it does understand why. We will speak later about this condition. At present we will speak of joy when it is active and voluntary and arises from things that are distinct and clear.

2. Joy may arise from six kinds of good things or blessings: temporal, natural, sensual, moral, supernatural, and spiritual. As we speak of these in order, we will presuppose one fundamental truth, which will be like a staff we should always lean on as we progress. This truth is threefold: the will must never rejoice except only in what is to the honor and glory of God; the greatest honor we can show to God is that of serving him according to the perfection of the Gospels; anything that has nothing to do with this is of no value.

CHAPTER 17
Joy with respect to temporal blessings.

1. The first kind of blessing of which we have spoken is temporal. By temporal blessings we mean riches, rank, office, children, relatives, marriages, and other things that people desire. All of these are things in which the will may rejoice. It is vain for people to rejoice in temporal blessings, for if a person were the better servant of God for being rich, he ought to rejoice in riches. But in fact they are instead a cause for his giving offense to God, even as the wise man of Proverbs teaches in these words: Son, if you are rich, you will not be free from sin.

2. Temporal blessings do not necessarily of themselves cause sin, yet through frailty the heart of mankind habitually clings to them and fails God (and to fail God is sin). The wise man of Proverbs says: You will not be free from sin.

For this reason in the Gospels the Lord described riches as thorns to show that one who touches them with the will, will be wounded by some sin. The exclamation that he makes in the Gospels, "How hard it is for those who have riches to enter the Kingdom of heaven"—meaning those who have joy in riches—clearly shows that a person must not rejoice in riches since by doing so he exposes himself to great peril. David, in order to withdraw us from this peril, said also: If riches abound, do not set your heart on them.

3. Solomon possessed great riches, and knowing well what they were, he said: All things that are under the sun are vanity of vanities, vexation of spirit, and vain solicitude of the mind. One who loves riches, he said, will reap no fruit from them. He adds that riches when held onto hurt their owner. We see this in the Gospels, where God said to the man who rejoiced because he had kept many fruits for many years: Fool, this night your soul will be required of you to give account for it, and whose will be what you have provided? Finally, David teaches us the same: Let us have no envy when our neighbor becomes rich, for it will profit him nothing in the life to come. By this he means that we might have pity on him instead.

4. It follows that one must rejoice in riches neither when he has them nor when his brother or sister has them, unless they help them to serve God. If ever one is allowed to rejoice in them, it will be when they are used in God's service, for otherwise no profit will come from them. The same is true of other blessings (titles, offices, and so on), in all of which it is vain to rejoice if God is not the better

served because of them and the way to eternal life is not made more secure. As the Lord says: If a person gains the whole world, he may yet lose his soul. So there is nothing in which to rejoice except in the fact that God is better served.

5. Neither is there cause for rejoicing in one's children because they are numerous or rich or endowed with natural graces and talents and the good things of fortune, but only if they serve God. David's son Absalom found neither his beauty nor his riches nor his lineage of any service to him because he did not serve God. Therefore it was vain for David to rejoice in such a son.

6. Therefore, though all things smile on a person and all that he does turns out prosperously, he ought to have misgivings rather than to rejoice, for these things increase the peril of his forgetting God. This is why in Ecclesiastes Solomon says that he was cautious: Laughter I counted error and to rejoicing I said—Why are you vainly deceived? Which is as though he had said: When things smiled on me I counted it error and deception to rejoice in them. It is a great error and folly on the part of a person to rejoice when things are bright and pleasant for him, not knowing of a certainty that eternal good will come to him as a result of them.

7. The heart of the fool, says the wise man of Proverbs, is where there is mirth, but that of the wise is where there is sorrow. Mirth blinds the heart and does not allow it to consider things and ponder them, but sadness makes a person open his eyes and look at the profit and the harm they bring.

8. It would therefore be vanity for a woman or her husband to rejoice in their marriage when they do not know clearly

that they are serving God better because of it. We must not set our rejoicings on anything other than what tends to God's service, for joy that is not according to God can bring the soul no profit.

— CHAPTER 18 —

The evils that may come to the soul by rejoicing in temporal blessings.

1. If we had to describe the evils that encompass the soul when it sets the affections of its will on temporal blessings, neither ink nor paper would suffice us and our time would be too short. From small beginnings a person may obtain great evils and destroy great blessings, just as a spark of fire if not quenched may enkindle great fires that set the world ablaze.

2. All these evils have their root and origin in one important evil of a privative kind that is contained in this joy: withdrawal from God. Just as in the soul that is united in its will with God all blessings come, when it withdraws itself from him for love of created things, evils and disasters beset it in proportion to the joy and affection it sets on created things. Therefore a soul may expect the evils that assail it to be greater or less according to the greater or lesser degree of its withdrawal from God.

3. This privative evil, out of which other privative and positive evils arise, has four degrees, each one worse than the other.

When the soul arrives at the fourth degree, it will have compassed all the evils and depravities that arise. Moses in Deuteronomy portrayed these four evils in these words: The beloved grew fat and kicked. He grew fat and became swollen and gross. He forsook God his Maker and departed from God his Salvation.

4. The soul's growing fat, which it loved before it actually grew fat, indicates absorption in the joy of created things. Out of that joy the first degree of this evil arises, that is, going backward, which is a certain blunting of the mind with regard to God, and an obscuring of the blessings of God like the obscuring of the air by mist so that it cannot be clearly illumined by the light of the sun. Precisely when the spiritual person sets his rejoicing on anything and gives rein to his desire for foolish things, he becomes blind as to God and the simple intelligence of his judgment becomes clouded.

5. Holiness and good judgment are not enough to keep a person from falling into this evil if one gives way to longing for or rejoicing in temporal things. This is why God warned us by uttering these words through Moses: You shall take no gifts, which blind even the prudent. This was addressed particularly to judges, for judges must keep their judgment clear and alert. And this they will be unable to do if they covet and rejoice in gifts. This is also why God commanded Moses to appoint judges from among those who hated greed. The reason the prophet Samuel was always such an upright and enlightened judge is that he never accepted a gift from anyone.

6. The second degree of this privative evil arises from the first: He grew fat and became swollen and gross. So the second degree is giving reign to the will through acquiring greater freedom in temporal things. This arises in the soul from its having first given rein to rejoicing; for through giving way to it, the soul has become swollen with it. This brings with it great evils: The soul withdraws itself from the things of God and from holy practices, and it takes no pleasure in them because it takes pleasure in other things and devotes itself continually to imperfections and follies and joys and vain pleasures.

7. When this second degree reaches its climax, it withdraws a person wholly from the practices that he followed continually, and makes his whole mind and desire to be given to things of the world. Those affected by this second degree not only have their judgment and understanding darkened so that like those who are in the first degree they cannot recognize truth and justice, but they are also weak and lukewarm and careless in acquiring knowledge of truth and justice, and in practicing them. They withdraw themselves more and more from justice and virtues, since their will reaches out more and more in affection for created things.

8. Therefore, the characteristics of those who are in this second degree are great lukewarmness in spiritual things and failure to do their duty by them. They practice them out of formality or out of compulsion or out of the habit that they have formed of practicing them, rather than because they love them.

9. The third degree of this privative evil is falling completely away from God, neglecting to fulfill his law in order not

to lose worldly things and blessings, and relapsing into the greatest sin through greed. This third degree is described in the next words from the passage quoted above: He forsook God his Maker.

10. This degree includes all who have the faculties of the soul absorbed in things of the world and in riches and commerce, in such a way that they care nothing for fulfilling the obligations of God's law. They are forgetful and dull with respect to what touches their salvation, and they have a correspondingly greater ardor and shrewdness with respect to things of the world. In the Gospels Christ calls them children of this world and says of them that they are more prudent and discriminating in their affairs than are the children of light in their own. In God's business they are as nothing, whereas in the world's business they are everything.

11. These are the truly greedy, those who have extended and dispersed their desire and joy on created things, and this with such affection that they cannot be satisfied. On the contrary, their desire and their thirst grow all the more because they are farther withdrawn from the only source that could satisfy them, which is God. It is of these that God himself spoke through Jeremiah in these words: They have forsaken me, who am the fountain of living water, and they have dug themselves broken cisterns that can hold no water.

12. This is why the greedy person finds nothing among created things with which he can quench his thirst, but only what increases it. These are the persons who fall into countless

kinds of sin through love of temporal blessings, and the evils that afflict them are innumerable.

13. The fourth degree of this privative evil is indicated in the last words of our passage, which says: And he departed from God his Salvation. Those of the third degree end up at this one. By not setting the heart on the law of God because of temporal blessings, the greedy person's soul departs far from God in his memory, understanding, and will, forgetting him as though he were not his God. This happens because he has made for himself a god of money and of temporal blessings. This fourth degree leads a person so far as to forget God and to set his heart, which he should properly have set on God, on money, as though he had no other god.

14. To this fourth degree belong those do not who hesitate to subject divine and supernatural things to temporal things, when they ought to do the contrary and subject temporal things to God. Among these were Balaam, who sold the grace that God had given to him, and Simon the Magician, who thought to value the grace of God in terms of money and desired to buy it. In doing this he showed a greater esteem for money; and he thought there were those who similarly esteemed it, and would give grace for money.

15. There are many nowadays who in other ways belong to this fourth degree. Their reason is darkened to spiritual things by greed. They serve money and not God and are influenced by money and not by God. They put the cost of a thing first, and not its divine worth and reward, and in many ways make money their principal god and end, and place it ahead of the final end, which is God.

16. To this last degree belong also those miserable souls who are so greatly in love with their own goods that they take them for their god, so much so that they do not hesitate to sacrifice their lives for them when they see that this god of theirs is suffering some temporal harm. When they can no longer hope for anything from him he gives them despair and death. Those whom he does not pursue to this last evil of death he condemns to a dying life in the grief of anxiety and many other miseries.

CHAPTER 19

The benefits that come to the soul by withdrawing from joy in temporal things.

1. The spiritual person, then, must see carefully to it that his heart and his rejoicing do not begin to lay hold on temporal things. Let him never be self-confident because his attachment is small, and fail to uproot it instantly because he thinks that he will do so later. If, when it is so small and in its beginnings, he does not have the courage to make an end of it, how does he suppose and presume that he will be able to do so when it is great and more deeply rooted? Our Lord said in the Gospels: He that is unfaithful in little will be unfaithful also in much.

2. Although one might not do this for God's sake and that of the obligations of Christian perfection, he should nevertheless do it because of the temporal advantages that result from it, to say nothing of the spiritual advantages, and he should

free his heart completely from all rejoicing in the things mentioned above. He will acquire freedom of soul, clarity of reason, rest, tranquility, peaceful confidence in God, and a true reverence and worship of God that comes from the will. He will find greater joy and recreation in created things through his detachment from them. He will therefore enjoy them differently from one who is attached to them, and over such a one he will have a great advantage and superiority. Renouncing and purging such joy leave the judgment clear, even as the mists leave the air clear when they are scattered.

3. The spiritual person rejoices in all things—since his joy is dependent on none of them—as if he had them all. The other, looking on them with a particular sense of ownership, loses all the pleasure of them. The former, having none of them in his heart, possesses them all. The latter, inasmuch as he has something of them through the attachment of his will, neither has nor possesses anything; rather, it is they that have possessed his heart, and he is, so to speak, a sorrowing captive. The spiritual person, then, must restrain the first motion of his heart towards created things, remembering the premise that we have set down, that there is nothing in which a person should rejoice except in his service of God and in his striving for God's glory and honor in all things.

4. There is another important benefit in detaching oneself from created things: It leaves the heart free for God. The soul gains even from the temporal standpoint, for one joy that the soul renounces for love of God and for the perfection of the gospel, God promises to give it a hundred in this life.

CHAPTER 20

The evils that may come to the soul by rejoicing in the good things of nature.

1.   The spiritual and physical evils that directly and effectively come to the soul when it sets its rejoicing on the good things of nature are reduced to six principal evils.

The first is vainglory, presumption, pride, and disesteem of one's neighbor; for a person cannot cast eyes of esteem on one thing without taking them from the rest. From this follows a real disesteem for everything else. From this real contempt it is easy to fall into an intentional and voluntary contempt for all these other things, not only in the heart, but also in speech.

The second evil is the moving of the senses to complacency and sensual delight and lust.

The third evil comes from falling into adulation and vain praise, in which is deception and vanity.

The fourth evil is of a general kind: It is a serious blunting of the reason and the spiritual sense, such as is effected by rejoicing in temporal good things. In one way, indeed, it is much worse. As the good things of nature are more closely connected with mankind than are temporal good things, the joy that they give leaves an effect on the senses more readily and more effectively, and deadens them more completely.

From this arises the fifth evil, which is distraction of the mind by created things.

Out of this come lukewarmness and weakness of spirit, which is the sixth evil.

2. Returning now to speak of the second evil, which contains within itself innumerable other evils, it is impossible to describe with the pen or to express in words the lengths to which it can go. Every day we hear of its causing numerous deaths, the loss of honor by many, the commission of many insults, the dissipation of much wealth, strife, adultery, rape, and fornication, and the fall of many holy persons. How far the poison of this evil penetrates!

3. Who does not drink, either little or much, from this golden chalice of the Babylonian woman of Revelation? She seats herself on that great beast that had seven heads and ten crowns, signifying that there is hardly anyone, high or low, saint or sinner, who does not come to drink of her wine. She seizes on all estates of mankind, even on the highest and noblest estate—the service of the sanctuary and the holy priesthood—setting her abominable cup, as Daniel says, in the holy place, and leaving scarcely a single strong man without making him drink, either little or much, from the wine of this chalice, which is vain rejoicing. For this reason Holy Scripture says that all the kings of the earth have become drunken with this wine, for few will be found, however holy they may have been, who have not been to some extent stupefied and bewildered by drinking of the joy and pleasure of natural graces and beauty.

4. This phrase "have become drunken" should be noted. However little a person may drink of the wine of this rejoicing, it at once takes hold on the heart and stupefies it and works the evil of darkening the reason, as does wine to those who have been corrupted by it. If some antidote is

not at once taken against this poison, by which it may be quickly expelled, the life of the soul is endangered. Its spiritual weakness will increase, bringing it to such a condition that it will be like Samson when his eyes were put out and the hair of his first strength was cut off, and like Samson it will see itself grinding in the mills, a captive among its enemies.

5. Let us conclude, then, by giving the instruction necessary to counteract this poison. Let it be this: As soon as you feel your heart moved by vain joy in the good things of nature, remember how vain and perilous a thing it is to rejoice in anything except God's service. As the wise man of Proverbs says: Do not look on the wine when its color is red and when it shines in the glass; it enters pleasantly and bites like a viper, and sheds abroad poison like a cobra.

CHAPTER 21
The benefits that come to the soul by not rejoicing in the good things of nature.

1. Many benefits come to the soul through withdrawing its heart from this rejoicing. Besides preparing itself for the love of God and the other virtues, it makes a direct way for its own humility and for a general charity toward its neighbors. As it is not led into affection for anyone by the apparently good yet deceitful things of nature, the soul remains free and able to love them all rationally and spiritually, as God wills them to be loved.

2.　Another excellent benefit that comes to the soul from renouncing this kind of rejoicing is that it fulfils and keeps the counsel that Our Savior gives us through Matthew: Let one who will follow me deny himself. This the soul could not do at all if it were to set its rejoicing on the good things of nature, for one who makes any account of himself neither denies himself nor follows Christ.

3.　There is another great benefit in renouncing this kind of rejoicing, which is that it produces great tranquility in the soul, empties it of distractions, and brings recollection to the senses, especially to the eyes. By guarding its doors, which are the senses, the soul guards itself safely and increases its tranquility and purity.

4.　There is another benefit of no less importance to those who have become proficient in mortifying this kind of rejoicing, which is that evil things and the knowledge of them neither make an impression on them nor stain them as they do to those who delight in these things. Renouncing and mortifying this rejoicing results in spiritual cleanness of soul and body. The soul comes to have an angelical conformity with God, and becomes, both in spirit and in body, a worthy temple of the Holy Spirit. This cannot happen if the heart rejoices in natural graces and good things.

5.　Another benefit of a general kind follows, which is that besides freeing ourselves from evils and dangers, we are delivered also from countless vanities.

6.　From these benefits follows the last, which is a generosity of the soul, as necessary to the service of God as is freedom of spirit, by which temptations are easily vanquished and trials faithfully endured, and also by which the virtues grow and become prosperous.

CHAPTER 22

The third good thing in which the will may rejoice.

1. We have next to turn to rejoicing with respect to the good things of the senses, which is the third kind of good thing in which we said that the will may rejoice. By the good things of the senses we here understand everything in this life that can be grasped by the senses of sight, hearing, smell, taste or touch, and by the interior fashioning of mental reflections, all of which things pertain to the physical senses, interior and exterior.

2. The senses may receive pleasure and delight, either from the spirit by means of some communication that it receives from God interiorly, or from outward things communicated to them.

3. I wish, therefore, to propose a test of when delights of the senses are profitable and when they are not: Whenever a person hears music, sees pleasant things, is conscious of sweet perfumes, tastes delicious things, or feels soft touches, if his thought and the affection of his will are at once centered on God and if that thought of God gives him more pleasure than the movement of the senses that causes it, and except for that he finds no pleasure in it, this is a sign that he is

receiving benefit from it and that this thing of the senses is a help to his spirit. In this way such things may be used, for then such things of the senses serve the end for which God created and gave them: that he should be the better loved and known because of them.

4. Whatever pleasure coming from the senses presents itself to the spiritual person, whether it comes to him by chance or by design, he must make use of it only for God, lifting up to him the rejoicing of his soul so that his rejoicing may be useful and profitable and perfect. All rejoicing that does not imply renouncing and bringing to nothing every other kind of rejoicing, even if it is over something apparently lofty, is vain and unprofitable and is a hindrance toward the union of the will in God.

CHAPTER 23

The benefits that come to the soul by not rejoicing in things of the senses.

1. The soul derives marvelous benefits from self-denial in this rejoicing. Some of these are spiritual and some temporal.

2. First, by restraining its rejoicing as to things of the senses, the soul is restored from the distraction into which it has fallen through excessive use of the senses and is recollected in God.

3. Second, what was sensual becomes spiritual, and what was animal becomes rational. The soul is journeying from

a human life to an angelical inheritance. Instead of being temporal and human, it becomes celestial and divine. One who seeks the pleasure of things of the senses and sets his rejoicing on them neither merits nor deserves any name other than those that we have given him—that is, sensual, animal, and temporal. In the same way, when he exalts his rejoicing above these things of the senses, he merits those other names—that is, spiritual and celestial.

4. Although the use of the senses and the power of sensuality are opposites, it follows that when one kind of power diminishes and comes to an end, the opposite kind, whose growth was hindered by the first kind, increases. So when the spirit is perfected (which is the higher part of the soul and the part that has communications with God and receives his communications), it merits all these attributes that we have described, since it is perfected in the heavenly and spiritual gifts and blessings of God.

5. Both these things are proved by Paul, who calls the sensual person (that is, the person who directs the practice of his will solely to sense) the animal man, who does not perceive the things of God. But this other man, who lifts up his will to God, he calls the spiritual man, saying that this man penetrates and judges all things, even the deep things of God. Therefore the soul gains in this the marvelous benefit of a disposition well able to receive the blessings and spiritual gifts of God.

6. The third benefit is that the pleasures and the rejoicing of the will in temporal matters are greatly increased. If you deny yourself one joy, the Lord will give you a hundred

times more joy in this life, both spiritually and temporally. In the same manner, for one joy that you have in the things of the senses, you will have a hundred times more affliction and misery. Through the eye that is purged from the joys of sight there comes to the soul a spiritual joy, directed to God in all things that it sees. Through the ear that is purged from the joy of hearing, the soul has a hundred times more spiritual joy directed to God in all that it hears. And the same is true with the other senses when they are purged.

7. Therefore, to one who is pure, all things, whether high or low, are an occasion of greater good and further purity. It follows that the impure person is apt to derive evil from things both high and low because of his impurity. The person who lives no more according to the senses, being pure in heart, finds in all things a knowledge of God that is joyful and pleasant, chaste, pure, spiritual, glad, and loving.

8. There is no need to speak of the blessings of glory that in the life to come result from renouncing these joys. Apart from the fact that the physical gifts of the life of glory, such as agility and clarity, will be much more excellent than in those souls who have not denied themselves, there will be an increase in the essential glory of the soul corresponding to its love of God, for whose sake it has renounced the things of the senses. As Paul says: For every momentary, fleeting joy that has been renounced there will be laid up an exceeding weight of eternal glory.

CHAPTER 24

The fourth kind of good in which the will may rejoice.

1. The fourth kind of good in which the will may rejoice is moral. By this we mean the virtues insofar as these are moral, the practice of any virtue, the practice of works of mercy, the keeping of God's law and of that of the common good, and the putting into practice of all good intentions and inclinations.

2. God loves moral good so much that just because Solomon asked him for wisdom so that he might teach his people, govern them justly, and bring them up in good customs, God himself was greatly pleased with him and told him that because he had asked for wisdom to that end, he would receive it, and that he would also receive what he had not asked for, that is, riches and honor, so that no king either in the past or in the future would be like him.

3. But, although the Christian should rejoice in the moral good that he possesses and in the good works of a temporal kind that he does, since they lead to temporal blessings, he must not allow his joy to stop at this first stage. Since he has the light of faith, in which he hopes for eternal life, without which nothing that pertains to this life and the next will be of any value to him, he must move on to the second stage, rejoicing principally and solely in that by doing these works for the love of God he will gain eternal life. The Christian, then, must rejoice, not in performing

good works and following good customs, but in doing them for the love of God alone, without respect to anything else whatsoever. Seeing that only good works that are done to serve God will have the greater reward in glory, the greater will be the confusion in the presence of God of those who have done them for other reasons.

4. The Christian, then, if he will direct his rejoicing to God with regard to moral good, must realize that the value of his good works, fasts, alms, penances, and so on, is based, not on the number or the quality of them, but on the love of God that inspires him to do them. They are the more excellent when they are performed with a purer and sincerer love of God and when there is less in them of self-interest, joy, pleasure, consolation, and praise, whether with reference to this world or to the next.

CHAPTER 25

The seven evils that may come to the soul by rejoicing in moral good.

1. The principal evils into which a person may fall through vain rejoicing in his good works and habits I find to be seven; and they are harmful because they are spiritual.

2. The first evil is vanity, pride, vainglory and presumption; for we cannot rejoice in our works without esteeming them. From this arise boasting and similar things, as is said of the Pharisee in the Gospel story, who prayed and congratulated

himself before God, boasting that he fasted and did other good works.

3. The second evil is usually linked with the first: It is our judging others, by comparison with ourselves, as wicked and imperfect, when it seems to us that their acts and good works are inferior to our own; we esteem them the less highly in our hearts, and at times also in our speech. This evil was also that of the Pharisee, for in his prayer he said: I thank you that I am not as other people are—robbers, unjust, and adulterers. So that by one single act he fell into both these evils, esteeming himself and despising others.

4. The third evil is that as we look for pleasure in our good works, we usually perform them only when we see that some pleasure and praise will result from them. So, as Christ says, we do everything so that we might be seen by others, and we do not work only for the love of God.

5. The fourth evil follows from this: Those who do these things will have no reward from God, since they have desired in this life to have joy or consolation or honor or some other kind of interest as a result of their good works. The Savior says that in this such persons have received their reward. In the good works that some persons perform, may it not be said that they are worshiping themselves more than God? This is certainly true if they perform them for the reason described and otherwise would not perform them at all.

6. But leaving these aside, how many are there who fall into these evils in their good works in many ways? Some wish to be praised, others wish to be thanked, and others enumerate their good works and desire that this person and that will know

of them, and indeed the whole world. Sometimes they desire an intermediary to present their alms or to perform some of their other charitable deeds, so that more may be known of them. This is the sounding of the trumpet that vain persons do, says the Savior in the Gospel, and that is why they will have no reward from God for their works.

7. In order to flee from this evil, such persons must hide their good works so that God alone may see them, and must not desire anyone to take notice of them. They must hide them, not only from others, but also even from themselves. That is to say, they must find no satisfaction in them nor esteem them as if they were of some worth. This is what Our Lord meant when he said: Let your left hand not know what your right hand is doing.

8. The fifth of these evils is that such persons make no progress on the road of perfection, for they are attached to the pleasure and consolation that they find in their good works. When they find no pleasure and consolation in their good works and practices, which ordinarily happens when God desires to lead them on by giving them the dry bread of the mature and taking from them the milk of babes, in order to prove their strength and to purge their delicate appetites so that they may be able to enjoy the food of grown persons, they commonly faint and cease to persevere because their good works give them no pleasure. When any mortification comes to these persons, they die to their good works and cease to practice them, and as a result they lose their perseverance, in which are found sweetness of spirit and interior consolation.

9.   The sixth of these evils is that such persons commonly deceive themselves, thinking that the things that give them pleasure must be better than those that give them none. They praise and esteem the former and depreciate the latter. Yet as a rule the works by which a person is most greatly mortified (especially when he is not proficient in perfection) are more acceptable and precious in the sight of God because of the self-denial that he must observe in performing them than those in which he finds consolation and which may easily be an occasion of self-seeking.

10.   The seventh evil is that to the extent that a person does not stifle vain rejoicing in moral works, he is incapable of receiving reasonable instruction about the good works that he should perform. Such persons as this are greatly weakened in charity toward God and their neighbor; the self-love with respect to their good works in which they indulge causes their charity to grow cold.

CHAPTER 26

The benefits that come to the soul through not rejoicing in moral good.

1.   Great benefits come to the soul when it does not desire to set the vain rejoicing of its will on moral good. In the first place, it is freed from falling into many temptations and deceits of the devil that are involved in rejoicing in good works. We may understand this by what is said in Job: He

sleeps under the shadow, in the covert of the reed and in moist places. This he applies to the devil, who deceives the soul in the moisture of rejoicing and in the vanity of the reed—that is, in vain works.

2. It is no wonder that the soul is secretly deceived by the devil in this rejoicing, for apart altogether from his suggestions, vain rejoicing is itself deception. This is especially true when there is any boasting of heart concerning these good works. The soul that purges itself from this rejoicing is freed from this.

3. The second benefit is that the soul performs good works with greater deliberation and perfection than it can if it does them for the passion of joy and pleasure. Since it acts under the influence of pleasure, and since pleasure is variable, being much stronger in some natures than in others, it follows that when this pleasure ceases both the action and its purpose cease, important though they may be. To such persons the joy that they have in their work is its soul and strength. When the joy is quenched, the work ceases and perishes, and they no longer persevere. It is of such persons that Christ says: They receive the word with joy, and then the devil takes it away from them for fear that they should persevere. This is because they have no strength and no roots except in their joy. Therefore to withdraw their will from this rejoicing is the cause of their perseverance and success.

4. The third benefit is divine—it is that when vain joy in good works is quenched, the soul becomes poor in spirit. This is one of the blessings spoken of by the Son of God when he

says: Blessed are the poor in spirit, for theirs is the Kingdom of heaven.

5.   The fourth benefit is that one who denies himself this joy will be meek, humble, and prudent in his actions. He will not act impetuously and rapidly through being impelled by the wrath and greed that belong to joy.

6.   The fifth benefit is that he becomes pleasing to God and man and is freed from spiritual sloth, gluttony, avarice, spiritual envy, and a thousand other vices.

CHAPTER 27
The fifth kind of good in which the will may rejoice.

1.   We now turn to the fifth kind of good thing in which the soul may rejoice, which is the supernatural. By this term we mean all the gifts and graces given freely by God that transcend natural virtue and capacity. Of these are the gifts of wisdom and knowledge that God gave to Solomon, and the graces of which Paul speaks—that is, faith, gifts of healing, the working of miracles, prophecy, knowledge and discernment of spirits, interpretation of words, and the gift of tongues.

2.   The practice of these has an intimate relation with the profit of mankind, and it is to this end that God gives them. As Paul says: The spirit is given to no one except for the profit of the rest; this is to be understood to mean these graces. But the use and practice of spiritual graces has to do with

the soul and God alone, and with God and the soul, in the communion of understanding and will. There is a difference in their object, since spiritual graces have to do only with the Creator and the soul, whereas supernatural graces have to do with created things, and furthermore differ in substance and therefore in operation.

3. In order to purge ourselves of vain joy in supernatural graces and gifts, it is good here to notice two types of benefits that are included in this kind of gift—that is, temporal and spiritual. The temporal benefits are the healing of infirmities, the receiving of their sight by the blind, the raising of the dead, the casting out of devils, prophesying concerning the future so that people may pay attention to themselves, and other things of the kind. The spiritual and eternal benefit is that God is known and served through these good works by the one who performs them or by those in whom and in whose presence they are performed.

4. With respect to the first kind of benefit—that is, the temporal—supernatural works and miracles merit little or no rejoicing on the part of the soul. Without the second kind of benefit they are of little or no importance, since they are not in themselves a means for uniting the soul with God as charity is. Supernatural works and graces may be performed by those who are not in a state of grace and charity, whether they truly give thanks and attribute their gifts to God, as did the wicked prophet Balaam, and Solomon, or whether they perform them falsely through the agency of the devil, as did Simon the Magician, or by means of other secrets of nature. If any of these works and

marvels were to be of any profit to the one who worked them, they would be true works given by God.

5.   One should rejoice, not when one has such graces and makes use of them, but when one reaps from them the second spiritual fruit, that is, that of serving God in them with true charity, for in this is the fruit of eternal life. For this cause Our Savior rebuked the disciples who were rejoicing because they cast out devils, saying: Do not rejoice in that devils are subject to you, but rather because your names are written in the book of life. By this it is understood that a person should not rejoice except when he is walking in the way of life, which he may do by performing good works in charity.

6.   Where is the profit and what is the worth in the sight of God of anything that is not love of God? Love is not perfect if it is not strong and discreet in purging the will of joy in all things, and if it is not set on doing the will of God alone. In this manner the will is united with God through supernatural good things.

CHAPTER 28

The evils that come to the soul when it rejoices in this kind of good.

1.   Three principal evils, it seems to me, may come to the soul when it sets its rejoicing on supernatural good. The first is that it may deceive and be deceived. The second is that it

may fall away from the faith. The third is that it may indulge in vainglory or some other such vanity.

2.   As to the first of these, it is easy to deceive others and to deceive oneself by rejoicing in this kind of operation. The reason is that in order to know which of these operations are false and which are true, and how and at what time they should be practiced, much counsel and much light from God are needed, both of which are greatly impeded by joy in these operations and esteem for them. This is for two reasons: first, because joy blunts and obscures the judgment; and second, because, when a person has joy in these things, not only does he the more quickly become eager for them, but he is also the more impelled to practice them out of the proper season.

3.   When God gives these gifts and graces he gives light by which to see them, and at what times and in what ways to use them. Yet these souls, through the attachment and imperfection that they may have with regard to them, may greatly err by not using them with the perfection that God desires of them and in the way and at the time that he wills. We read that Balaam desired to do this when, going against the will of God, he determined to go and curse the people of Israel, for which reason God was angry and purposed to slay him. James and John desired to call down fire from heaven on the Samaritans because they did not give lodging to Our Savior, and for this he rebuked them.

4.   These persons were determined to perform these works when it was not proper for them to do so, led by a certain imperfect passion that was inherent in their esteem for these works.

When no such imperfection exists, the soul is moved to perform acts of virtue only in the manner in which God so moves it, and in his time, and until then it is not right to perform them.

5. From these passages we see that the evil of this rejoicing not only leads people to make wicked and perverse use of these God-given graces, as did Balaam, but also it even leads them to use these graces without having been given them by God. When the devil sees them attached to these things, he opens a wide field to them, gives them abundant material, and interferes with them in many ways. At that they spread their sails and become shamelessly audacious in the freedom with which they work these marvels.

6. One who has supernatural gifts and graces ought to refrain from practicing them and from rejoicing in so doing, and he ought not to practice them. God, who gives himself to such persons by supernatural means for the profit of his Church and of its members, will move them also supernaturally in such a manner and at such time as he desires.

7. From this first evil may proceed the second, which is falling away from the faith. This can happen in two ways. The first is with respect to others. When a person sets out unseasonably and needlessly to perform a marvel or a mighty work, apart from the fact that this is tempting God, which is a great sin, it may be that he will not succeed and will engender in people's hearts discredit and contempt for the faith. Although at times such persons may succeed because for other reasons and purposes God so wills it, as in the case of Saul's witch of Endor (if it actually was Samuel who appeared on that

occasion), they will not always succeed. Even when they do so, they go astray nonetheless and are blameworthy for having used these graces when it was not right.

8. The second manner in which we may fall away is in ourselves and has respect to the merit of faith. If a person makes much account of these miracles, he ceases to lean on the substantial practice of faith. Where signs and witnesses abound, there is less merit in believing. God never works these marvels except when they are really necessary for belief.

9. Therefore, so that his disciples should not be without merit, though they had experienced his resurrection, he did many things before he showed himself to them so that they would believe him without seeing him. To Mary Magdalene, first of all, he showed the empty tomb, and afterward told the angels to speak to her (for, as Paul says, faith comes by hearing). This he did so that having heard, she would believe before she saw. He first sent to tell his disciples, with the women, and afterward they went to see the tomb. And as to those who went to Emmaus, he first of all enkindled their hearts in faith so that they might see him, not revealing himself to them as he walked.

10. Finally he rebuked them all because they did not believe those who announced his resurrection to them. He rebuked Thomas, who demanded to have the evidence of his wounds, by telling him that those who do not see him and yet believe him are blessed.

11. It is not God's will to work miracles. When he works them, he does so, so to speak, because he cannot do otherwise. That is why he rebuked the Pharisees, because they did not

believe except through signs: Unless you see marvels and signs, you do not believe. Those who love to rejoice in these supernatural works lose much in the matter of faith.

12. The third evil is that because of their joy in these works, some persons commonly fall into vainglory or some other vanity. When their joy in these wonders is not purely in God and for God, it is vanity. This is evident in the rebuke that Our Lord gave to the disciples because they had rejoiced that devils were subject to them. If their joy had not been vain, he would not have rebuked them.

CHAPTER 29
Two benefits that come to the soul from renouncing joy in the supernatural graces.

1. By being delivered from these three evils through the renouncing of this joy, the soul acquires two excellent benefits. The first is that it magnifies and exalts God; the second is that it exalts itself. God exalts the soul in two ways: first, by withdrawing the heart and the joy of the will from all that is not God, in order to set them on him alone. This David signified when he said: Man will obtain a lofty heart, and God will be exalted. For when the heart is raised above all things, the soul is exalted above them all.

2. Because in this way the soul centers itself in God alone, God is exalted and magnified when he reveals to the soul his excellence and greatness. For in this elevation of joy,

God bears witness of who he himself is. This cannot be done unless the will is emptied of joy and consolation with respect to all things. As David said: Be still and know that I am God. Again David says: In a desert land, dry and pathless, I have appeared before you to see your power and your glory. The more and the greater things a person despises for the sake of another, the more he esteems and exalts the other.

3.   Furthermore, God is exalted in the second way when the will is withdrawn from this kind of operation. The more we believe and serve God without testimonies and signs, the more he is exalted by the soul, for it believes more concerning God than signs and miracles can ever demonstrate.

4.   The second benefit in which the soul is exalted consists in this, that withdrawing the will from all desire for apparent signs and testimonies, it is exalted in purest faith, which God increases and infuses within it much more intensely. Together with this, he increases in it the other two theological virtues, which are charity and hope, of which the soul enjoys the highest divine knowledge by means of faith. It enjoys great delight of love by means of charity, by which the will rejoices in nothing else than in the living God, and it enjoys satisfaction in the memory by means of hope. All this is a wondrous benefit that leads essentially and directly to the perfect union of the soul with God.

~ CHAPTER 30 ~

The sixth kind of good in which the will may rejoice.

1. In speaking of the sixth kind of good, we need to turn to the good things of the spirit, which are those that are of the greatest service to this end. It is quite an ordinary occurrence that some persons, because of their lack of knowledge, make use of spiritual things with respect only to the senses and leave the spirit empty. There will scarcely be anyone whose spirit is not to a considerable degree corrupted by sweetness of sense.

2. By good things of the spirit I mean all those that influence and aid the soul in divine things and in its communication with God and in God's communications to the soul.

3. Beginning by making a division between these supreme kinds of good, the good things of the spirit are of two kinds: One kind is delectable and the other painful. Each of these kinds is also of two types. The delectable kind consists of clear things that are distinctly understood, and also of things that are not understood clearly or distinctly. The painful kind, also, may be of clear and distinct things, or of dark and confused things.

4. Between all these we may also make distinctions with respect to the faculties of the soul. Some kinds of spiritual good, being of knowledge, pertain to the understanding. Others, being of affection, pertain to the will. Still others, inasmuch as they are imaginary, pertain to the memory.

CHAPTER 31
The spiritual good things that bring joy to the will.

1. We can reduce all the kinds of good that can distinctly cause joy in the will to four: motive, provocative, directive, and perfective. First, the motive kind—that is, images and portraits of saints, oratories, and ceremonies.

2. As touching images and portraits, there may be much vanity and vain rejoicing in these. Though they are most important for divine worship and most necessary to move the will to devotion, as is shown by the approval given to them and the use made of them by the Church (for which reason it is always good to make use of them in order to awaken our lukewarmness), there are many persons who rejoice in the painting and decoration of them rather than in what they represent.

3. The truly devout person sets his devotion principally on what is invisible. He needs few images and uses few, and chooses those that harmonize with the Divine rather than with the human, clothing them, and with them himself, in the garments of the world to come, and following its fashions rather than those of this world. Not only does an image pertaining to this world in no way influence his desire, but also it does not even lead him to think of this world, in spite of his having before his eyes something worldly. Nor is his heart attached to the images that he uses; if they are taken from him, he grieves little.

4. The truly devout person seeks within himself the living image, which is Christ crucified, for whose sake he would even desire that everything should be taken from him and he should have nothing. Although it is good to have such images as assist the soul to greater devotion (for which reason it is those that move it most that must always be chosen), it is something far removed from perfection to be so greatly attached to them as to possess them with attachment, so that if they are taken away from the soul, it becomes sad.

5. Let the soul be sure that the more closely it is attached to an image, the less its devotion and prayer will mount to God. It is true that some are more appropriate than others and excite devotion more than others, so it is good for this reason alone to be more attached to some than to others. Yet there must be none of the attachment and affection that I have described. Otherwise, what has to sustain the spirit in its flight to God, in total forgetfulness, will be wholly occupied by the senses, and the soul will be completely immersed in a delight afforded it by what are only instruments. I use these instruments, but only to assist me in devotion. On account of my imperfection, they may well serve me as a hindrance no less than may affection and attachment to anything else.

CHAPTER 32

The use of images in perceiving God and spiritual things.

1. There is much that might be said of the stupidity that many persons display with regard to images. Their foolishness reaches such a point that some of them place more confidence in one kind of image than in another, believing that God will hear them more readily because of these than because of those, even when both represent the same thing, such as when there are two of Christ or two of Our Lady. This is because they have more affection for the one kind of workmanship than for the other.

2. Such a display implies the crudest ideas concerning interaction with God and the worship and honor that are owed to him, which has solely to do with the faith and the purity of heart of the one who prays. If God sometimes grants more favors by means of one image than by another of the same kind, it is not because there is more virtue to this effect in one than in another (however much difference there may be in their workmanship), but because some persons awaken their own devotion better by one than by another. If they had the same devotion for the one as for the other (or even without the use of either), they would receive the same favors from God.

3. God does not do this because of the image, which in itself is no more than a painted thing, but because of the devotion and faith that the person has toward the saint it represents.

When God grants certain favors and works miracles, he does so as a rule by means of images that are not well carved or cunningly formed or painted, so that the faithful may attribute nothing to the figure or the painting.

4. Furthermore, Our Lord frequently grants these favors by means of remote and solitary images. One reason for this is that the effort necessary to journey to them causes the affections to be increased and makes the act of prayer more earnest. Another reason is that we may withdraw ourselves from noise and from other persons when we pray, even as the Lord did. Therefore one who makes a pilgrimage does well if he makes it at a time when no others are doing so, even though the time may be unusual. I would never advise him to make a pilgrimage when a great multitude is doing so, for as a rule, on these occasions, people return in a state of greater distraction than when they went.

5. Many set out on pilgrimages and make them for recreation rather than for devotion. Where there is devotion and faith, then, any image will suffice, but if there is none, none will suffice. Our Savior was a living image in the world, and yet those who had no faith, even though they went about with him and saw his wondrous works, derived no benefit from them. This was why, as the Gospel writer says, he did few mighty works in his own country.

6. I desire also to speak here of certain supernatural effects that certain images sometimes produce on particular persons. To certain images God gives a particular spiritual influence on such persons, so that the figure of the image and the devotion it causes remain fixed in the mind, and the person

has them always present before him. So when he suddenly thinks of the image, the spiritual influence that works on him is of the same kind as when he saw it—sometimes it is less, but sometimes it is even greater. Yet from another image, although it may be of more perfect workmanship, he will not obtain the same spiritual effect.

7.   Many persons have devotion to one kind of workmanship rather than to another, and to some they will have no more than a natural inclination and affection, just as we prefer seeing one person's face to another's. They will naturally become more attracted to a particular image, and will keep it more vividly in their imagination, even though it may not be as beautiful as others, just because their nature is attracted to the kind of form and figure that it represents. Some persons will think that the affection that they have for such or such an image is devotion, whereas it will perhaps be no more than natural inclination and affection.

8.   It may happen that when some persons look at an image they will see it move, or make signs and gestures and indications, or speak. These are quite frequently good and true effects, produced by God either to increase devotion or so that the soul may have some support on which to lean because it is somewhat weak, and so that it may not be distracted. Yet frequently they are produced by the devil in order to cause deception and harm. We will therefore give instruction concerning this in the chapter following.

CHAPTER 33

Images can be used to direct the soul to God.

1. Just as images are of great benefit for remembering God and the saints and for moving the will to devotion when they are used in the proper way, they will lead to great error if, when supernatural happenings occur in connection with them, the soul should not be able to conduct itself as is fitting for its journey to God. One of the means by which the devil easily lays hold on incautious souls and obstructs the way of spiritual truth for them is the use of extraordinary and supernatural happenings, transforming himself into an angel of light so that he may deceive. In those means that serve for our relief and help, the shrewd devil contrives to hide himself in order to catch us when we are least prepared. Therefore it is concerning good things that the good soul must always have the greatest misgivings, for evil things bear their own testimony with them.

2. There are three evils that may happen to the soul in this connection, that is, its being hindered from soaring upward to God, its using images in an unworthy and ignorant manner, and its being deceived by them through natural or supernatural means. To purify the rejoicing of the will in them and by means of them to lead the soul to God, for which reason the church recommends their use, I desire here to set down only one warning that will apply to all these things. The warning is this: Since images serve us as a motive for invisible things, we must strive to set the motive and the affection and the rejoicing of our will only on what in fact they represent.

3. Let the faithful soul, then, be careful that when he sees an image, he does not desire that his senses should be absorbed by it whether the image is physical or in the mind, whether beautifully made, whether richly adorned, whether the devotion that it causes is of the senses or of spirit, whether it produces supernatural manifestations or not. The soul must on no account set store by these things, nor even regard them, but must raise up its mind from the image to what it represents, centering the sweetness and rejoicing of its will, together with the prayer and devotion of its spirit, on God or on the saint who is being invoked. What pertains to the living reality and to the spirit should not be usurped by the senses and by the painted object.

4. If the soul does this it will not be deceived. An image that would cause the soul devotion by supernatural means will now do so more abundantly, since the soul will now go with its affections directly to God. For whenever God grants these and other favors, he does so by inclining the joy of the will to what is invisible, and this he wishes us also to do.

CHAPTER 34
Motives for goodness.

1. The spiritual person may find as great imperfection in setting his pleasure and rejoicing on images as on other physical and temporal things, and perhaps even more perilous imperfection. When a person says that the objects

of his rejoicing are holy, he feels more secure and does not fear to cling to them in a natural way. Such a person is sometimes greatly deceived, thinking himself to be full of devotion because he takes pleasure in holy things, when perhaps this is due only to his natural desire and temperament, which lead him to this just as they lead him to other things.

2. Some persons never tire of adding to their oratories images of one kind and then another, and take pleasure in the order in which they set them out so that these oratories may be well adorned and pleasing to behold. Yet they love God no more when their oratories are ornate than when they are simple—in fact, they love him less, since the pleasure that they set on their painted adornments is stolen from the living reality.

3. It is true that those who have images and treat them with a lack of decency and reverence are worthy of severe rebuke, as are those who have images so ill-carved that they take away devotion rather than produce it. But what does that have to do with the attachment that you have for these outward adornments and decorations, when your senses are absorbed by them in such a way that your heart is hindered from journeying to God, and from loving him and forgetting all things for love of him? If you fail in the latter aim for the sake of the former, not only will God not esteem you for it, but also he will even chasten you for not having sought his pleasure in all things rather than your own.

4. This you may clearly gather from the description of the celebration that the people of Jerusalem made for Our Lord

when he entered their city. They received him with songs and with branches, but the Lord wept, for their hearts were far removed from him and they paid him reverence only with outward adornments and signs. We may say of them that they were making a festival for themselves rather than for God.

5. This is done nowadays by many, who, when there is some solemn festival in a place are apt to rejoice because of the pleasure they themselves will find in it—whether in seeing or in being seen, or whether in eating or in some other selfish thing—rather than rejoicing at being acceptable to God. They are giving no pleasure to God by these inclinations. Especially is this so when those who celebrate festivals invent ridiculous and undevout things to intersperse in them so that they may incite people to laughter, causing them greater distraction.

6. What shall I say of persons who celebrate festivals for reasons connected with their own interests? They alone, and God who sees them, know if their desire is set on such interests rather than on God's service. When they act in any of these ways, let them realize that they are making festivals in their own honor rather than in God's.

7. Many who take part in God's festivals will be enjoying themselves even while God is angry with them, as he was with the children of Israel when they made a festival and sang and danced before their idol, thinking that they were keeping a festival in honor of God. Or as with the person who entered the wedding feast without the proper garments, the king commanded that he should be thrown

into outer darkness, bound hand and foot. By this we can see how poorly God thinks of this irreverence in assemblies that are held for his service.

8. How many festivals, O my God, are made to you by people to the devil's advantage rather than to yours! The devil takes delight in them, because such gatherings bring him business, as they might to a trader. How often will you say concerning them: This people honors me with their lips alone, but their heart is far from me, for they serve me from a wrong cause! The only reason to serve God must be that he is who he is.

9. Returning now to oratories, let us consider those who think themselves devout. Many of these center their pleasure on their oratory and its adornments, to such an extent that they squander on them all the time that they should be spending in prayer to God and in interior recollection. They cannot see that by not arranging their oratory with a view to the interior recollection and peace of the soul, they are as much distracted by it as by anything else.

CHAPTER 35
The way in which oratories and churches should be used.

1. It is certainly permitted and even expedient for beginners to find sweetness and pleasure in images, oratories, and other visible objects of devotion, since they have not yet

weaned their desire from things of the world, so that they can leave one pleasure for the other. They are like a child holding something in one of its hands; to make it loosen its hold on it we give it something else to hold in the other hand in case it should cry because both hands are empty.

2. But the spiritual person who would make progress must strip himself of all the pleasures and desires in which the will can rejoice. Pure spirituality is bound little to any of those objects, but only to interior recollection and mental conversation with God. Although he makes use of images and oratories, he does so only fleetingly; his spirit at once comes to rest in God and he forgets all things of the senses.

3. Although it is best to pray where there is the most decency, one should choose the place where sense and spirit are least hindered from journeying to God. Here we should consider the answer Our Savior gave the Samaritan woman when she asked him which was the more fitting place in which to pray, the temple or the mountain. He answered her that true prayer is not connected with the mountain or the temple, but those who worship the Father and are pleasing to him are those who worship him in spirit and in truth.

4. Although churches and pleasant places are set apart and furnished for prayer (for a church must not be used for anything else), for a matter as intimate as conversing with God one should choose a place that gives the senses the least occupation and the least encouragement.

5. This is why Our Savior chose solitary places for prayer. He chose places that lift up the soul to God, such as mountains,

which are lifted up above the earth and are usually bare, offering no occasion for exercising the senses.

6. The truly spiritual person, then, is never tied to a place of prayer because of its suitability in this way or in that. Rather, in order to achieve interior recollection and forget everything, he chooses the places that are most free from distractions, withdrawing his attention from them so that he may be able to rejoice in his God and be far removed from all things created.

CHAPTER 36

Three places that God uses to move the will to devotion.

1. I can think of three kinds of place that God uses to move the will to devotion. The first consists in a pleasing arrangement of gardens or of trees, which by means of quiet solitude, naturally awaken devotion. It is beneficial to use such places if they at once lead the will to God and cause it to forget the places themselves, for spiritual sweetness and satisfaction are found only in interior recollection.

2. The second kind is of a more special nature, for it relates to certain places (not necessarily deserts, but any places whatever) where God is accustomed to grant to a few special persons delectable spiritual favors. Such a place attracts the heart of the person who has received a favor there and sometimes gives him a yearning to return to it. When he goes there, what happened to him before is not repeated,

since this is not within his control. God grants these favors when and how and where he pleases, without being tied to any place or time or to the free will of the person to whom he grants them.

3.   Yet it is good to go and pray in such places at times if the desire is free from attachment to them. This is for three reasons: First, because although God is not bound to any place, it would seem that he has willed to be praised by a soul in the place where he has granted it a favor. Second, because in that place the soul is more mindful to give thanks to God for what it has received there. Third, because by remembering that favor the soul's devotion is the more keenly awakened.

4.   It is for these reasons that a person should go to such places, and not because he thinks that God is bound to grant him favors there and is unable to grant them wherever he wills. For the soul is a fitter and more comely place for God than any physical place. Thus we read in Holy Scripture that Abraham built an altar in the place where God appeared to him and invoked his holy name there, and later he returned from Egypt by the same road and called on God once more at the same altar.

5.   The third kind consists of certain special places that God chooses so that he may be called on and served there, such as Mount Sinai, where he gave the law to Moses; the place that he showed Abraham, so that he might sacrifice his son there; and Mount Horeb, where he appeared to Elijah.

6.   The reason God chooses these places rather than others, so that he may be praised there, only he knows. What we

must know is that it is all for our advantage, and that he will hear our prayers there. He will hear our prayers no matter where we pray to him with perfect faith, but there is much greater opportunity for us to be heard in places dedicated to his service.

CHAPTER 37

*Other motives for prayer that
many persons use.*

1. I wish to speak of the ceremonies of which many persons make use nowadays with indiscreet devotion, attributing such effectiveness and faith to the ways in which they desire to perform their devotions and prayers, that they believe that if they fail to the slightest extent in them, or go beyond their limits, God will not be served by them nor will he hear them. They place more reliance on these methods and kinds of ceremony than on the reality of their prayer, and in this they greatly offend and displease God.

2. I refer, for example, to a Mass at which there must be so many candles, neither more nor fewer; which has to be said by the priest in such or such a way; and must be at such or such a time, and neither sooner nor later; and must be after a certain day, neither sooner nor later; and the prayers and stations must be made at such and such times, with such or such ceremonies, and neither sooner nor later nor in any other manner; and the person who makes them must have

such or such qualities or qualifications. There are persons who think that if any of these details that they have laid down are missing, nothing is accomplished.

3. What is intolerable is that certain persons desire to feel some effect in themselves, or to have their petitions fulfilled, or to know that the purpose of these ceremonious prayers of theirs will be accomplished. This is nothing less than to tempt God and to anger him greatly.

CHAPTER 38

The joy and strength of the will must be directed to God through devotions.

1. Let these persons know that the more reliance they place on these ceremonies the less confidence they have in God, and that they will not obtain of God what they desire. There are certain persons who pray for their own ends rather than for the honor of God. They multiply a large number of petitions for something, when it would be better for them to substitute others of greater importance to them, such as the true cleansing of their consciences, and a real application to things concerning their own salvation. In this way they would obtain what is of the greatest importance to them, and at the same time all the other things that are good for them. The Lord promised this through the Gospel writer, saying: Seek first and principally the Kingdom of God and his righteousness, and all these other things will be added unto you.

2.   This is the seeking and asking that is most pleasing to God. In order to obtain the fulfillment of the petitions that we have in our hearts, there is no better way than to direct the energy of our prayer to the thing that most pleases God. Then not only will he give what we ask of him, which is salvation, but also what he sees to be right and good for us even if we do not pray for it.

3.   David makes this clear in the psalm where he says: The Lord is near those who call on him in truth, who beg him for the things that are true in the highest degree, such as salvation. Of these he then says: God will fulfill the will of those who fear him, and will hear their cries and will spare them. God is the guardian of those who truly love him. The nearness to God of which David here speaks is nothing other than his being ready to satisfy them and grant them even what has not passed through their minds to ask.

4.   Because Solomon did well in asking God for a thing that was pleasing to him—that is, wisdom to lead and rule his people righteously—God answered him in these words: Because more than anything else you desired wisdom, and did not ask for victory over and the death of your enemies, nor riches, nor long life, I will not only give you the wisdom that you ask for to rule my people righteously, but I will also give you what you have not asked for—that is, riches and substance and glory—so that neither before you nor after you will there be any king like you.

5.   Let not the will be set on ceremonies and forms of prayer other than those that Christ taught us. When his disciples asked him to teach them to pray, he told them everything

that is necessary for the Eternal Father to hear us, since he knew the Father's nature so well.

6. Yet all that he taught them was the Lord's Prayer, with its seven petitions, in which are included all our needs, both spiritual and temporal. He did not teach them many other kinds of prayer, either in words or in ceremonies. On the contrary, he told them that when they prayed they ought not to desire to speak much, since our heavenly Father knows well what we need. He charged them only, but with great insistence, to persevere in prayer (that is, in the Lord's Prayer). He did not teach a variety of petitions, but rather that our petitions should be repeated frequently and with fervor and care. They contain all that is God's will and all that we need.

7. There are only two ceremonies that he taught us to use in our prayers: We are to pray in the secret place of our chamber, where without noise and without paying attention to anyone we can pray with the most perfect and pure heart. He said: When you pray, enter into your chamber and shut the door and pray. Or else he taught us to go to a solitary and desert place, as he himself did, and at the best and quietest time of night.

8. So there is no reason to fix any limit of time, or any appointed days, or to set apart one time more than another for our devotions, neither is there any reason to use other forms in our words and prayers. For all are reduced to the one prayer that we have described—that is, the Lord's Prayer.

CHAPTER 39

Teaching others is a spiritual practice rather than a vocal one.

1. The second kind of distinct and delectable good in which the will may rejoice vainly is what provokes or persuades us to serve God and which we have called provocative. This type includes preachers. We might speak of it in two ways, that is, as affecting the preachers themselves and as affecting their hearers. As regards both, both must direct the rejoicing of their will to God with respect to this practice.

2. If the preacher is to benefit his people and not shame himself with vain joy and presumption, he must know that preaching is a spiritual practice rather than a vocal one. Although it is practiced by means of outward words, its power and effectiveness do not reside in these but in the inward spirit. Therefore, however lofty the doctrine that he preaches and however choice the rhetoric and sublime the style that he uses, these things bring no more benefit than is present in his spirit. Although it is true that the word of God is of itself effective—David said: He will give to his voice a voice of strength—yet fire, which has the property of burning, will not burn when the material is not prepared.

From Dr. Pao, I learned to be
an Iscapable servant.

From Pastor Dennis Bestul, I learned
to sow the seeds and let the fruits
grow automatically, which means
the Holy Spirit is doing His work,

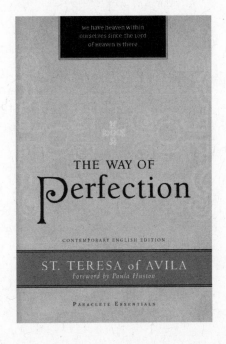

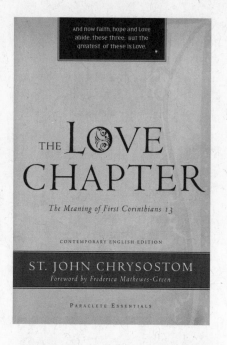

and now faith, hope and Love abide, these three; but the greatest of these is Love.

THE LOVE CHAPTER

The Meaning of First Corinthians 13

CONTEMPORARY ENGLISH EDITION

ST. JOHN CHRYSOSTOM

Foreword by Frederica Mathewes-Green

PARACLETE ESSENTIALS